**LIBRARY
OF
ADVENTIST THEOLOGY**

The Cross of Christ

Series Editors:

George R. Knight
Woodrow W. Whidden II

Other books by George R. Knight include:

A Search for Identity
A Brief History of Seventh-day Adventists
Ellen White's World
Exploring Ecclesiastes and the Song of Solomon
Exploring Galatians and Ephesians
Exploring Hebrews
Exploring Mark
If I Were the Devil
Joseph Bates
Meeting Ellen White
Organizing for Mission
Reading Ellen White
Walking With Ellen White
Walking With Paul in the Book of Romans

To order, call **1-800-765-6955**.

Visit us at
www.reviewandherald.com
for information on other Review and Herald® products.

THE CROSS OF CHRIST

God's Work for Us

GEORGE R. KNIGHT

REVIEW AND HERALD® PUBLISHING ASSOCIATION
Since 1861 | www.reviewandherald.com

Copyright © 2008 by Review and Herald® Publishing Association
Published by Review and Herald® Publishing Association, Hagerstown, MD 21741-1119

All rights reserved. No portion of this book may be reproduced, stored in a retrieval system, or transmitted in any form or by any means (electronic, mechanical, photocopy, recording, scanning, or other), except for brief quotations in critical reviews or articles, without the prior written permission of the publisher.

The Review and Herald® Publishing Association publishes biblically-based materials for spiritual, physical, and mental growth and Christian discipleship.

The author assumes full responsibility for the accuracy of all facts and quotations as cited in this book.

An earlier edition of *The Cross of Christ: God's Work for Us* was published in 1990 as *My Gripe With God: A Study of Divine Justice and the Problem of the Cross*, by Review and Herald Publishing Association.

Unless otherwise noted, Bible texts in this book are from the Revised Standard Version of the Bible, copyrighted 1946, 1952 © 1971, 1973.

Texts credited to NEB are from *The New English Bible*. © The Delegates of the Oxford University Press and the Syndics of the Cambridge University Press 1961, 1970. Reprinted by permission.

Texts credited to NIV are from the *Holy Bible, New International Version*. Copyright © 1973, 1978, 1984, International Bible Society. Used by permission of Zondervan Bible Publishers.

This book was
Edited by Gerald Wheeler
Designed by Trent Truman
Cover photo: © ernestking/istockphoto.com
Interior designed by Heather Rogers
Typeset: Bembo 11/13

PRINTED IN U.S.A.

12　11　10　09　08　　　　　　5　4　3　2　1

Library of Congress Cataloging-in-Publication Data
Knight, George R.
　　The Cross of Christ: God's work for us/George R. Knight.
　　　　p. cm. — (Library of Adventist theology; bk. 1
　　Includes bibliographical reference and index.
　　　　1. Atonement—Seventh-Day Adventists. 2. Seventh-Day Adventists—Doctrines. I. Title
　　BT265.3.K55 2008
　　232' .3—dc22

ISBN 978-0-8280-2067-1

Dedicated to

Gil and Gail Valentine
special people who are devoted to Christ and His cross

Contents

A Word to the Reader 9

Chapter 1 My Problem With God 13
An Upsetting Bible Story • More Perturbing Stories • What Kind of God Would Create Our Kind of World? • Distrust of God Is Central to Scripture • God's Solution Seems to Play Into the Devil's Hands • God Is in Trouble • A Solution That Even God Can't Explain

Chapter 2 God's Problem With Me 28
Fig Leaves and Swimming Pools • Alienation and Estrangement • Slavery at Its Worst • A Dirtier Than Dirt Defilement • A More Powerful Bondage Than Sin • The Wrath of God • Perspective

Chapter 3 The Bible's Most Disgusting Teaching 44
The Old Testament Foundation • The Crucified God • The Problem of the Innocent Suffering for the Guilty • Why Couldn't God Forgive Without the Death of Jesus on the Cross? • The Unlovable Cross • Perspective

Chapter 4 God in Search of Rebels 61
Propitiation • Redemption • Justification • Reconciliation • Cleansing • Perspective

Chapter 5 Jesus' Real Temptation and the "Godforsakenness" of the Cross 81
Christ's Self-emptying • Overcoming Where Adam Failed • The Death of Temptation • It Is Finished • But It Is Obviously Not Finished

**Chapter 6 The Universe's Problem With God
and the Reason for the Millennium** 103
The Climax of History, the World's Longest Battle, and God's Judgment on Sin • The Millennium and the Judgment "on" God • The Verdict "for" God and the Apocalyptic Doxologies • It Is Really Finished

Chapter 7 Radical Faith's Response to the Cross 122
Radical Faith • The Death of a "Rebel" and the Birth of a "Saint" • The Cross and Daily Living • The Cross and the Life of the Church • The Cross and Personal Tragedy

A Final Word to the Reader 141

Index of Names and Topics 143

Index of Biblical References 150

A Word to the Reader

The problem of sin and the atoning work of Christ stands at the very center of Christianity, yet Seventh-day Adventists have written few books that even attempt to span its full range. Most Adventist writing on the work of Christ has focused on His heavenly ministry.[1] Such studies are needed, but treatments providing broader contextual understanding of that ministry are important also.

A major purpose of *The Cross of Christ* is to provide a book on the atonement that utilizes Adventist insights and covers the broad spectrum of topics raised by the problem of sin and God's work in Christ to resolve that problem.

The book begins with the questions I struggled with concerning God's justice when, as a 19-year-old agnostic, I first read the Bible. From that point it moves to (1) the results of sin in the human realm, (2) God's solution for reversing those consequences, and (3) how that solution is being worked out through the life and death of Christ.

The final two chapters cover (1) the universe's judgment on God's solution and (2) the human response to salvation. I will be treating the human side of salvation more fully in the companion volume to this one—*Sin and Salvation*. Both books deal with the plan of salvation, but this one focuses more on what God accomplishes for people, while the second will emphasize humanity's application of God's solution.

After grappling with the topic of Christ's atoning work for a while, I began to develop gut-level feelings that perhaps I should have selected a more manageable subject. I began to understand what Ellen White meant when she wrote that "it will take the whole of eternity for man to understand the plan of redemption." Also I discovered the truthfulness of Sydney Cave's assertion that "no one can write of Christ's work without a sense of utter inadequacy."[2]

In spite of those rather threatening realizations, I pushed ahead, knowing that whatever I wrote would fall far short of dealing with the immense topic.

Not only is Christ's atoning work complex and important; it is also controversial. Christian theologians have split into several camps regarding the significance of the cross and the other aspects of Christ's work. Despite the variations, theologies of the work of Christ tend to divide into a few rather well-defined camps.

Perhaps the most basic dividing line between competing interpretations of the atonement forms along the boundary of the proper relationship between Scripture and human reason. Two varying approaches seem to account for most of the important divergences.

The first begins with the Bible, which it interprets rationally while seeking to be faithful to the redemptive symbols.

The second one starts with a set of *a priori* rationalistic presuppositions, which it utilizes in an attempt to make good human sense out of the words of Scripture. The result of the second method has generally been to explain away many of the rather straightforward biblical symbols to make them more palatable to the modern mind. Seventh-day Adventist interpreters have used both methods. *The Cross of Christ* sympathizes with the first approach.

The present book treats the work of Christ within the framework of a cosmic conflict. The problem of sin is much more than a human crisis. It affects the entire universe. In fact, the real issue in the great struggle between good and evil is not the justification of humanity, but rather of God. Human justification is a by-product of God's. Thus, *The Cross of Christ* places the cross in a universal context.

Beyond the theme of cosmic conflict, the present book treats the atonement as a process that began at the time sin entered the universe and will continue until the close of the millennium. We should, therefore, think of the atonement as a line rather than a single point, even though the crucifixion of Christ is the turning point in the conflict between God and Satan.

The present book primarily covers its topic from the perspective of biblical categories (such as sacrifice, redemption, reconciliation, and so on), rather than from the viewpoint of the theological theories developed to explain the work of Christ.

On the other hand, even though the book's structure is not built around the theological categories, it treats all of the main theories of the atonement in relation to the scriptural framework that gives them meaning. Thus I will introduce the reader to the basic concepts that underlie the governmental, satisfaction, victory, and moral influence theories of the atonement.

I should also offer a word about style. The publisher wanted me to present the topic with as much human interest as possible, while my main burden was to develop the subject matter and write a book that was factually accurate. The result is something of a compromise, which I hope will edify the interested reader while also being responsible to the deeper concerns of the subject.

Three books especially helped me as I approached the atoning work of Christ.

Gustaf Aulén's *Christus Victor* uplifts the theme of Christ's victory as the focal point in the atonement.

The second volume was H. Wheeler Robinson's *Redemption and Revelation in the Actuality of History*. Robinson helped me see that the most fundamental criticism of Aulén's work is that he needed a deeper philosophy of history to give background to the work of Christ. He suggested that Aulén treated the result of Christ's work, but failed to capture the dynamic process that brought about the victory.[3]

The third book was Ellen White's *The Great Controversy*, part of a five-volume set that provides both the process and the philosophy of history that puts the atonement in cosmic perspective.[4]

The Cross of Christ is a book I have been "writing in my head" since I was a seminary student 40 years ago. Its themes form the framework of the only worldview that makes sense to me.

I am particularly indebted to two teachers who helped me visualize the significance of the cross of Christ: Carl Coffman, who enabled me to see that the cross is the center of every other Christian belief; and Edward Heppenstall, who taught me that the cross is the context of all theology and cosmic history.

An earlier edition of the present book appeared in 1990 under the title of *My Gripe With God: A Study in Divine Justice and the Problem of the Cross*. The new version has added sections on defilement and cleansing in chapters 2 and 4, respectively, and has tuned up and extended the treatment of the justification of God in chapter 4. Otherwise, outside of editorial changes, the content has remained mostly the same.

My debts in writing this book have been many. Special thanks go to Richard M. Davidson, Raoul Dederen, Robert M. Johnston, and Kenneth A. Strand for reading the entire manuscript of the initial publication. It was with a certain degree of anxiety that I placed my work into their exacting hands. They responded, however, with both encouragement and helpful suggestions. The book is better because of their input, and perhaps might have been even stronger if I would have followed all of their counsel. Joyce Werner and Madeline Johnston also should receive thanks for entering my handwritten manuscript into the computer.

Appreciation for the present version of the book goes to Mika Devoux, for providing a cleaned up computerized version of the scanned copy; to my wife Bonnie for entering the seemingly endless rounds of corrections into the computer; to Woodrow Whidden, for making helpful suggestions for revision, and to Gerald Wheeler and Jeannette Johnson, for guiding the book through the publication process.

I trust that *The Cross of Christ: God's Work for Us* will be a blessing to its readers as they grapple with a most complex topic in both their intellectual and their daily lives.

George R. Knight
Rogue River, Oregon

---

[1] See chapter 5, note 47, for a listing of major Adventist treatments of the heavenly ministry of Christ.

[2] Ellen G. White, MS 21, 1895; Sydney Cave, *The Doctrine of the Work of Christ* (Nashville: Cokesbury, 1937), p. 305.

[3] H. Wheeler Robinson, *Redemption and Revelation in the Actuality of History* (London: Nisbet, 1942), pp. 246, 247.

[4] See Ellen G. White, *The Desire of Ages* (Mountain View, Calif.: Pacific Press, 1940), pp. 761-764 for an excellent summary of aspects of her understanding.

Chapter 1

My Problem With God

Reading certain parts of the Bible makes me mad! Take that story of the prodigal son. The first time I read it I almost quit the Bible altogether. After all, it obviously comes to the wrong conclusion. Let me illustrate.

An Upsetting Bible Story

The story of the prodigal occurs in Luke 15—a chapter that deals with three kinds of lostness.

The parable of the lost sheep represents people who are lost through their own foolishness. They get lost because they don't watch where they are going. Sheep know they are lost, but aren't sure what to do about it.

The parable of the lost coin pictures those lost through no particular fault of their own. In fact, they don't even know they are lost. Sheep have a little spiritual sense (enough to know they are lost), but coins lack spiritual sense altogether.

The parable of the lost son presents a totally different picture. His is a story of willful disobedience and *rebellion*. He deliberately schemes to get lost. Sick and tired of the old man's rules and restrictions, he *orders* his father to give him his share of the inheritance. No sooner does he get the money than he heads to "a far country" where he can cut loose and live it up without having to feel guilty around his father.

The son differs from the coin in that he recognizes that he is lost. And unlike the sheep he knows how to get home. The whole point of the contrast in the three parables is that the son is *glad to be lost*. The last thing on his mind is to go home. After all, he is on the road to freedom.

This differing nature of the lostness of the son points to an interesting aspect of God's love. When the sheep and coin were lost, someone conducted a diligent search to find them. But when the son was lost, the father did not use his many servants to restrain him. Neither did he search after him. On the contrary, when the boy demanded his inheritance, the father gave it to him.

Now, it seems to me that a son is more valuable than a coin or a sheep. Why, then, was there no search? The answer lies in the nature of the son's lostness. His is a case of high-handed rebellion, not one of weakness or ignorance. The young man rejoiced in living the lost life, and the father was wise enough to realize that love cannot be forced. The wisest course was to let his son experience his rebellion and reap the results.

That, as you will recall, is exactly what happened. The Bible says that the son went to a far country, where he spent his father's money in "loose living." But things went wrong, and we soon find the young fellow drooling over swine's slop.

At that point he "came to himself" and decided to head back home. Perhaps, he mused, he could *work* there as a hired servant, since he was "no longer worthy" to be a son. The father, of course, would have none of that. He ran out and conferred full sonship on the repentant son. Then he threw a big party to celebrate the young man's return.

So far, so good. Up to this point in my first reading of the parable, I was still somewhat in harmony with its general lesson. But then I came to the airtight logic of the older son and began to see the unfairness in the father's approach.

Put yourself in the firstborn's shoes. He had been a faithful worker on the family ranch (all of which was now a part of his personal inheritance, since his younger brother had cashed in his share). His life had been tolerable, but not particularly pleasant.

Heading back to the house with dirt under his fingernails and sheep manure on his sandals, he suddenly hears the sounds of the party—all of it being paid for by his hard work. Inquiring as to the occasion, he comes face to face with a personal injustice.

His anger, it seemed to me, was more than justified. From a human point of view the older son had a good case. *This young degenerate, after all, has spent his share of the inheritance, and now he comes home to spend mine*, he thought. *And why rejoice because he has come back home? What else could he have done? He was broke, destitute, and starving!*

The father, of course, went out to his older son to explain, but the rationale must have seemed weak at best. After all, the older son had shown heroic moral fortitude. He had laboriously kept the father's rule and law for his entire life. "I didn't like it," he cried to his father, "but I did it anyway. I would have liked to have drunk it up and chased around with wild women like your other son, but I kept your stinking commandments and worked like a dog. And look who gets a party!" he wailed in self-pity (see verses 29, 30).

The reading of Luke 15 upset my moral sensibilities. An obvious injustice had taken place. Neither son got what he deserved. And isn't getting what one deserves a basic principle of justice?

I might have read the chapter "properly" if I had been raised as a Christian. But as a 19-year-old agnostic, my mind had not been indoctrinated into viewing the story in a certain way. Instead, I merely read the words for what they said—and went away questioning God's justice.

I had yet to learn that His justice and human justice are not the same; that divine love and human love are qualitatively different; and that normal people give others what they *deserve*, but that God always presents them with what they *need*.

But is that fair? Is it just? Is God really divvying up the rewards properly?

More Perturbing Stories

Those questions bring us to Matthew 20 and the parable of unjust rewards. You will recall that Jesus told a story about an employer who hired workers at the beginning of the day and promised them a day's wage. Later he went out and hired more laborers, going back to find still more each hour until the eleventh hour of the 12-hour workday.

It is the way that Jesus told the story that particularly upset me. He has the employer line up the workers in exactly the reverse order of how he had hired them. Then, in full view of the others, the employer pays those who worked only one hour a full day's pay.

Now what do you think went on in the minds of those who had spent the whole day on the job? They started multiplying. Anyone who has worked on fruit farms or in construction knows how the laborer's mind operates. "If those guys get one day's pay for one hour's work," so the logic runs, "we deserve 12 days' pay—that is, two weeks' earnings if you subtract out the Sabbaths. At last," they rejoiced, "we have discovered an employer who will allow us to get ahead."

Then came the bombshell. All received exactly the same pay! No wonder they grumbled. I was a young construction worker when I first read Matthew 20, and I grumbled with them. To me it was a travesty of justice.

My discovery that Jesus told the parable of the employer in Matthew

20 as a direct response to a question set forth by the disciples in Matthew 19:27 did not help assuage my rebellious feelings.

In that verse, in the wake of the refusal of the rich young ruler to leave all for Christ, Peter asked Jesus what he and the other disciples would get, since they had "left everything and followed" Him. Jesus responded in chapter 20 that they would receive no more than those who come into the kingdom at the last hour.

Once again I found myself face to face with the justice of God, and He wasn't coming out too shiny in my secular mind. I had still not grasped that God's love and justice differ from human love and justice. In our natural state, we hand people what they *deserve*, but God gives them what they *need*.

The basis of human justice is what the Romans called *lex talionis*—the law of retaliation, the law of the claw, an eye for an eye, a good for a good. People get what they deserve.

On the other hand, the basis of God's justice is what Paul called *grace*. The simplest definition of grace is unmerited favor. In other words, *grace means that people receive what they do not deserve*.

The whole concept of grace ought to raise questions about God's justice, especially if people are not getting their proper reward after striving so hard for it. Such a situation could make a person feel downright hateful.

The parable of the sheep and goats in Matthew 25 also raises sticky questions about divine justice. A reader can hardly miss the element of surprise in that great judgment parable. And one doesn't have to read the story too many times to discover that the Pharisees end up on the wrong side of the judgment.

The reader must keep in mind that the Pharisees had dedicated their entire lives to keeping every jot and tittle of God's law. They had a saying that Messiah (Christ) would come if Israel kept Torah (the law) perfectly for one day.[1] Thus they totally dedicated their lives to bringing about that day. As a result, they paid as tithe every tenth leaf of their garden herbs, would never touch an unclean thing, and had scores of laws on Sabbath observance in the belief that such external acts would be the standard of God's judgment.

But then at the "last trump," the parable runs, the Pharisees discover to their disgust that God was not playing the game according to their rules. The Lord was more concerned with the inward condition of their hearts as expressed in serving other people in disinterested love than He was in "sinless perfection." Their outward acts of Sabbathkeeping, carefulness with foods, and scrupulous tithe paying were important, of course, but only within the context of reflecting Christ's character of love and personal "caringness." That concrete, caring personalness, Jesus implied in Matthew 25, was the "one point" upon which the judgment turned.[2] As a result, a whole lot of people who did not measure up to the Pharisees' high moral standards entered the kingdom, while many of the Pharisees found themselves left on the outside.

That parable is scarcely one to encourage those who have dedicated their entire lives to obeying God's law down to its minutest point. In my mind's eye, I can see many of those listening to Christ questioning the justice of such a judgment scene. It was hardly the type of story engineered to bring people into line through wielding a "straight testimony." I imagine that many of His hearers must have grumbled because He was overturning the "old ways." And, they must have queried, "What kind of weak-kneed, namby-pamby kingdom could possibly arise from such teachings?"

In my first reading of Matthew 25 I had many of those feelings. How could anyone measure "squishy" standards like love? The Pharisees had something solid and ought to be rewarded accordingly. Grace—giving people what they don't deserve—could be the world's most dangerous teaching. Could God's basis of judgment really be trusted?

Other Bible passages that early led me to question God's justice were Genesis 4:1-7 and Romans 9:14-18.

The conclusion to the Cain and Abel episode particularly caught me by surprise. Coming into Christianity at that time through the Adventist gate, I thought for certain that vegetables had to be better than blood. God's recognition of Abel's offering seemed arbitrary at best. I didn't know it at the time, but I was coming to grips with the symbolism of one of the most unpopular teachings in Christian history—the substitutionary sacrifice of Christ. At any rate, the whole event left me with more questions about God than answers.

Romans 9:14-18 provided me with a different set of problems. In verse 15 Paul quoted God as saying, "I will have mercy on whom I have mercy, and I will have compassion on whom I have compassion." The apostle then turned around in verses 17 and 18 and said that God had hardened Pharaoh's heart so that He could demonstrate His power. "Who," I queried to myself, "is this God whom we are supposed to love? On what grounds can He save some and destroy others? Is the divine nature basically unjust and arbitrary? Can God really be trusted?"

Such were some of the questions of a 19-year-old first-time reader of the Bible. The issue of God's justice, of course, is not just a problem in the Bible. We face it in the daily world around us.

What Kind of God Would Create Our Kind of World?
One of the most unforgettable experiences in my life took place in 1968 in Galveston, Texas, where I pastored the local Adventist church. One morning I received a long-distance call asking me to visit a West Coast patient who recently had been admitted into the nationally recognized University of Texas Medical School's burn clinic.

I was little prepared for what I found when I arrived. My first glimpse of the patient found me staring at a 2-year-old toddler. The child was feeding himself by holding a spoon between the two largest toes of its right foot. You see, this baby had no arms. A closer look helped me realize the extent of his injuries. Frightfully burned at the age of 1, he had no lips, just teeth; no ears; no eyelids; and no hair.

I had come to encourage the mother, but in total emotional disarray I retreated to the hallway, where the mother found me and sought to comfort me somehow. Even after 40 years, tears fill my eyes when that image comes to mind.

What kind of a world do we live in? I, conceivably, could have understood it if one of my parishioners or even I had been so mutilated, because we had developed ugly traits of character, and, one could argue, "deserved it." But what justification was there for the suffering of an innocent child? What kind of a hellish planet do we live on? Where is the so-called God of love?

"Is He," asks Philip Yancey, "the cosmic Sadist who delights in watching us squirm?"[3]

The experience of the burned child is repeated millions of times each year. Such is the injustice at the microcosmic, individual level. But the problem has also macrocosmic aspects. Whole groups of people suffer in Auschwitzes and Buchenwalds and through Hiroshimas and Nagasakis. Nearly everyone is aware that Adolf Hitler's "final solution" to bring about his millennial Third Reich caused the cold-blooded destruction of 6 million Jews, but they generally forget or overlook that the same program took the lives of 600,000 Gypsies and more than 6 million Slavs. Yet even Hitler's achievements stand in the shadow of Joseph Stalin's accomplishment in eliminating up to 50 million of his own people, a story excruciatingly documented in Aleksandr Solzhenitsyn's massive three-volume *Gulag Archipelago*.

No wonder the book of Revelation has the souls under the altar cry out with a loud voice: "O Sovereign Lord, . . . how long before thou wilt judge and avenge our blood on those who dwell upon the earth?" (Rev. 6:10).

How long, O Lord, how long? If God is all-wise and all-powerful, why doesn't He clean up this mess? "Behold, I come quickly" (Rev. 22:7, KJV) is the reply, but after 2,000 years one wonders what "quickly" means. For century after century it seems as if the lid has popped off of hell.

Can we trust a God who allows the world to get into such a botched-up state? And how would you feel if the "God of surprises" ended up giving Hitler or Stalin or some mass murderer what he doesn't deserve—grace—in the final judgment?

Distrust of God Is Central to Scripture

My personal questions about God, the Bible, and the everyday world are not unique. Doubt and distrust stand at the very foundation of the human predicament, as reflected in Eve's experience recorded in Genesis 3. Verse 1 plainly states that Satan was "more subtle than any other wild creature that the Lord God had made." Satan never came up to Eve and announced himself as the devil, who intended to deceive her. Rather, he insidiously sowed doubts in her mind. "Did God say . . . ?" was his first point of attack with Eve.

He uses the same tactic today. If he can get us to doubt God's word (*if* He really said it), he has won the battle. Failing at that point, the enemy sought to convince Eve that God didn't really mean what He said ("You will not die"). Satan's third tactic was to get Eve to question God's goodness and positive intentions toward her, insinuating that He did not want her to partake of the fruit because He was trying to keep the best things for Himself—in other words, that God is essentially selfish (Gen. 3:5, 6).

Satan's aim with both Eve and us is to sow distrust and doubt. Eve's distrust led her to rebel against God. As a result, she chose her will rather than His, and then put her will into action by eating the forbidden fruit. Sin occurred first in her mind. Afterward it became an outward act. Eve's "children" have been doubting God ever since. Distrust of God stands at the very foundation of the sin crisis.

But such distrust is more than just an earthbound problem. For that reason, Paul can speak of "the spiritual hosts of wickedness in the heavenly places" (Eph. 6:12) and the need for God "to reconcile all things, whether on earth or in heaven," to Himself (Col. 1:20, NEB).

The Cross of Christ

The sin problem began in heaven when Lucifer became proud and sought to make himself "like the Most High" (Isa. 14:12-14; Eze. 28:17).[4] In his campaign for self-glorification, he cast aspersion on the character and intentions of God, creating doubt throughout the universe. Lucifer and his followers were eventually expelled from heaven. Through his successful temptation of Adam and Eve he became "the ruler of this world" (John 16:11). In that position he has continued to spread doubt concerning God and His goodness. He takes every opportunity to misrepresent God's character. The thing to note at this juncture, however, is that the problem of divine distrust is cosmic rather than restricted to one little planet in the vast universe.

At the core of Satan's temptation to Eve was the inference that God could not be trusted because He was arbitrary in prohibiting her from the tree in "the midst of the garden"—that His commandment was unfair. Beyond that, Satan implied that God was untrustworthy because He was more intent in looking out for His own welfare by restricting her actions than He was in protecting her interests. Such has been the thrust of the accuser's charges against God down through the ages.

In reality, Satan's actions in Genesis 3 were not as much aimed at tempting Eve as they were in attacking and discrediting God. Eve was not the real enemy. The conflict was not between the devil and humanity, but between the devil and God.

Satan has consistently aimed his attacks, as the seventeenth century Dutch jurist Hugo Grotius pointed out, at the authority of God's government and the moral order of His universe. An attack on the divine rule, Grotius held, was an attack on God's law. And without stable law, no kingdom can stand. Reverence for the divine law is central to God's cosmic rulership. If He hopes to rule the universe, claimed the jurist, God must maintain the authority of His government and the sanctity of His law.[5]

God's problem was complicated not only by Satan's charge that God's laws were arbitrary, but also by the devil's success in having tempted the first earthlings to rebel against God, to choose their own wills above His, and to act deliberately against His revealed commandment.

The Lord had announced to Eve that death would result from such rebellion. That decree has always been God's pronouncement against sin. "The wages of sin is death" (Rom. 6:23).

The dual facts of the necessity of cosmic moral stability and the divinely decreed death penalty for rebellion against the divine government placed God in a predicament, because His nature consisted of mercy as well as justice.

"The same God," Loraine Boettner writes, "who is a God of mercy and who in virtue of His mercy desires to save human souls, is also a God of justice and in virtue of His justice must punish sinners. . . . For Him to fail to punish sin would be for Him to remove the penalty against it, to consent to it or to become partaker in it, and therefore to violate His own nature and to destroy the moral order of the universe." Nor could God set aside His law, which was "an expression of His being," rather than an "arbitrary or whimsical pronouncement."[6]

In that context, Satan set off a new barrage of charges against the God who would like to forgive, but was "stuck" with enforcing the penalty of the broken law.

"In the opening of the great controversy," Ellen White penned, "Satan had declared that the law of God could not be obeyed, that justice was inconsistent with mercy, and that, should the law be broken, *it would be impossible for the sinner to be pardoned*. Every sin must meet its punishment, urged Satan; and *if God should remit the punishment of sin, He would not be a God of truth and justice*. When men broke the law of God, and defied His will, Satan exulted. It was proved, he declared, that the law could not be obeyed; man could not be forgiven. Because he, after his rebellion, had been banished from heaven, Satan claimed that the human race must be forever shut out from God's favor. *God could not be just, he urged, and yet show mercy to the sinner.*"[7]

Thus the God who gives people what they don't deserve was pitted against the universe's most persuasive and influential legalist. The issue was—and is—God's justice, and Satan's tactic has ever been the promotion of doubt in and distrust of the divine Being.

God's Solution Seems to Play Into the Devil's Hands

But God chose to ignore neither the law nor the penalty of the broken law. Thus, in order to forgive sinful beings, the Bible claims, He sent Jesus into the world both to live a life in perfect obedience to the law and to bear the penalty for human sins on the cross (Heb. 4:15; 1 Peter 2:24).

That solution, however, merely provided critics with more ammunition. Anselm of Canterbury (1033-1109) clearly recognized the problem. What justice, he asked, was there in giving the best of all men over to death on behalf of sinners? "*What man would not be judged worthy of condemnation if he were to condemn the innocent in order to let the guilty go free?*" If God "could not save sinners otherwise than by condemning the just, where is His omnipotence? And if He could, but would not, how do we defend His wisdom and justice?"[8]

A generation later the scholarly Peter Abelard (1079-1142) wrote: "How cruel and wicked it seems that anyone should demand the blood of an innocent person as the price for anything, or that it should in any way please him that an innocent man should be slain—still less that God should consider the death of his Son so agreeable that by it he should be reconciled to the whole world!"[9]

The issue would later cause problems for the Socinians in the sixteenth century. They pointed out that the Bible taught that "the soul that sins shall die. The son shall not suffer for the iniquity of the father, nor the father suffer for the iniquity of the son; the righteousness of the righteous shall be upon himself, and the wickedness of the wicked shall be upon himself" (Eze. 18:20).

The Socinians found a double immorality in the concept of substitutionary sacrifice: (1) it allowed the guilty to go unpunished, and (2) it punished the innocent.[10]

God Is in Trouble

Sin is not simply a human problem. It is a cosmic dilemma that falls upon God primarily and upon human beings only secondarily. While it is true that we are caught in the web of sin, it is just as true that the weight of the sin problem ultimately rests upon God. "By the very structure of the universe," H. Wheeler Robinson penned, "by the creation of a world meant to achieve the divine purpose, it is impossible for sin to be the concern of man alone. Sin, as a partial or temporary defeat of the divine purpose, concerns God."[11]

God is in a "death-grapple,"[12] not with "flesh and blood," but with "the spiritual hosts of wickedness in the heavenly places" (Eph. 6:12). It is a conflict that permits no halfway victories. There can be no compromise between the sinful and the holy. "In the 'strange war' into which Christ enters," Karl Heim writes, "there are only two possibilities: either Christ allows Himself to be entirely destroyed by the ruler of this world, or the ruler of this world is entirely destroyed by Him so that Christ is victorious on the whole front."[13]

The supreme aim of history is to rid the universe of sin through God's judgment of it. "At the deepest level," suggests Jürgen Moltmann, "the question of world history is the question of righteousness."[14]

The issue is not one of human righteousness, but of God's. That problem is central to the Bible. Abraham raised it when pleading with God over the fate of Sodom and Gomorrah: "Shall not the Judge of all the earth do right?" (Gen. 18:25). The book of Job deals with the question of divine justice at length, and the author of Psalm 73 questions why God allows the wicked to prosper. Most important, however, is Paul's wrestling with the complex issue of how God can be just and righteous and still be "the justifier of him which believeth in Jesus" (Rom. 3:26, KJV).

The plan of redemption is as important for God as it is for us. In fact, all is lost if God is not justified as righteous in the eyes of the universe. Human justification is a by-product of the divine justification.[15]

Ellen White writes that *"the plan of redemption had a yet broader and deeper purpose than the salvation of man. It was not for this alone that Christ came to the earth,"* but *". . . it was to vindicate the character of God before the universe. . . .* The act of Christ in dying for the salvation of man would not only make heaven accessible to men, but *before all the universe it would justify God and His Son in their dealing with the rebellion of Satan.* It would establish the perpetuity of the law of God and would reveal the nature and the results of sin."[16]

Thus the question of questions is not merely the future of humanity, but that of God Himself. Our future is bound up with His, and our justification is tied to His. God's moral government has been challenged, and He has faced rebellion both in heaven and earth. Daily life is a mess of suffering and frustration. And even God's plan of sending Christ to save us seems to raise as many questions as it answers.

A Solution That Even God Can't Explain

How would you handle the sin problem if you were God? I know what I would do. Being all-knowing (omniscient), I could be certain that rebels deserved to die, and being all-powerful (omnipotent), I could give them their just deserts. One wave of my fist, and no one would even find a trace of the devil and his cohorts. After all, right is right, and it would be my moral responsibility to take action in cleaning the mess up.

It is probably good for you (and the rest of creation) that I am not God. You see, I am too prone to force my way. When I see a problem and know the answer, it is all too easy for me to begin to push other individuals toward my solution before they "see the light." Such an attitude, I am sorry to confess, is more a result of my fleshly nature than of my sanctification.

When it comes to God, we need to remember that Satan's accusations never centered on God's inability to solve the sin problem through a show of power. Rather, the devil focused on the claim that God wasn't just in the use of His authority. It wasn't His lack of power, but the abuse of it, that was at issue.[17]

Seen in that light, a forceful solution to the sin problem would have only increased the distrust of God. The obey-Me-or-I'll-kill-you approach was a possibility for God, but He knew that it would have only spread the infection of fear, distrust, and disharmony that Satan had originated.

While the universe would live in fear if God acted too soon, it could interpret delay as weakness on His part. Caught on the horns of an impossible dilemma, God chose to face the sin problem on the basis of sufficient time. H. E. Guillebaud writes that "the fact that God has not yet destroyed Satan shows that He has very good reasons up till now for not doing so. He hates evil infinitely more than we can . . . , but He is infinitely wiser than we are, and He knows what is best."[18]

God could employ only those means consistent with His character. Fritz Guy has argued that one of the great mistakes in the history of theology has been to see God's power and omnipotence as His preeminent characteristic. "If Christian theology *really* believes that Jesus the Messiah is the supreme revelation of God," Guy suggests, then it will see God's love as the trait that determines how He deals with problems.[19]

Thus God in His love chose "voluntarily to impose certain restrictions upon his course of action. . . . The *Christian* understanding of the omnipotence of God is that of a God *who voluntarily" limits Himself*.[20]

As a result, God in His wisdom has allowed Satan's takeover of the world by "divine 'consent.'"[21] We read in *Patriarchs and Prophets* that the universe's inhabitants did not understand the nature and consequences of sin and would not have seen "the justice of God" if the Lord had destroyed Satan at the beginning of the rebellion. "Had he been immediately blotted out of existence, some would have served God from fear rather than from love." The deceiver would have been eradicated, but not the distrust and spirit of rebellion that he had championed. "For the good of the entire universe throughout ceaseless ages" God permitted Satan to "demonstrate the nature of his claims." "It was necessary for his plans to be fully developed, that their true nature and tendency might be seen by all. . . . *His own work must condemn him.*" The problem would be solved only when the whole universe saw the deceiver unmasked. Only then would "the justice and mercy of God and the immutability of His law . . . be forever placed beyond all question. *Satan's rebellion was to be a lesson to the universe through all coming ages.*"[22]

However, a demonstration of Satan's perversity, as important as that was, answered only half the problem, for the deceiver had accused God of being unjust in subtle ways. *The other half of the cosmic drama must be "an objective demonstration of the righteousness of God."* Not only must the evil be exposed, claims Leon Morris, but "the right must be vindicated."[23]

But *how* could God, under the shadow of the accuser's charges, best vindicate Himself in this subtle struggle? How could He eradicate evil without raising fear in His subjects that Satan was right after all? And how could He save rebellious sinners in a way that would be just?

God apparently knew that some things can't be explained satisfactorily. *He therefore chose not to answer Satan's accusations through rational argument or a full-blown "theology." Rather, He chose to demonstrate His love in action. That demonstration would highlight and bring to a climax the principles of both sides in the cosmic struggle between good and evil.*

God's demonstration, P. T. Forsyth suggested in the midst of the atrocities of World War I, must be historic, rather than theoretical. It must take place in the flow of world history. The divine self-justification for the existence of our kind of world must be "a practical establishment of His holy goodness in the face of everything. It must be something historic which enables us to believe in the last reality, deep rule, and final triumph of goodness *in spite of history*." No human reason can justify God in our chaotic world. His justification must flow from a historic demonstration of His love. And that took place on the cross of Calvary,[24] where God allowed Christ to become sin for us (2 Cor. 5:21) and to bear the penalty for the broken law (Gal. 3:13; Col. 2:14). It was at the cross that God in Christ "disarmed the principalities and powers" of evil and "made a public example of them, triumphing over them in him" (Col. 2:15). The cross of Christ displays to the universe, as nothing else could, both the love of God and the malignant hatred of Satan's kingdom.

The cross, as a portrayal of two sets of antagonistic principles, spoke louder than any possible verbal argument. *It is at Christ's cross that the principles of both God's and Satan's kingdoms are exhibited in their full maturity.* The cross clearly testifies that God "loved the world" (John 3:16; 1 John 4:10).

But, it is important to note, the cross does much more than demonstrate God's love. It also allows God to demonstrate and maintain His holiness.

C. S. Lewis caught a basic truth when he pointed out that someone wrote a poem called "Love Is Enough," while another person critiqued it briefly in the words "It isn't."[25] God's love operates in relationship to His holiness, which includes His separateness from and hatred of moral evil (sin).[26]

Love without holiness could easily be permissive with sin. Such love could forget its rules and penalties for the sake of harmony and forgiveness. It could change and bend to circumstances regardless of principle. Forsyth, however, is certainly correct when he noted that we might love a love that could change, "but we could not trust it, however intense. It is the holiness within love that is the ground of such trust . . . as makes religion. It is this holiness that enables us to meet the love of God with faith, and not merely with gladness; to trust it for ever." In other words, God's love is guaranteed to be unchangeable because of His holiness. Therefore, "any conception of God which exalts His Fatherhood [that is, forgiving love that fails to take into account the penalty of God's broken law] at the cost of His holiness . . . unsettles the moral . . . universe."[27]

It is of the utmost importance to recognize that God's great demonstration of love at the cross took place in relation to His holiness. Jesus displayed both when He bore our sins at Calvary (1 Peter 2:24). In the death of Jesus we see both divine love and divine judgment on sin, rebellion, and lawlessness. That historical event opened the way for (1) reconciliation between us and God and (2) the eventual destruction of sin from the universe.

In this chapter we have seen that the crisis of sin is God's problem, rather than being merely humanity's. Satan has cast doubts on God's justice and trustworthiness, and God, in His wisdom, is giving Satan time to work out the principles of his kingdom.

Chapter 2 treats the problems that sin has brought to humanity, while chapters 3 through 6 examine God's solution to the sin problem.

---

[1] *Babylonian Talmud*, Sanhedrin 97b; Shaggath 118b; *Jerusalem Talmud*, Taanith 64a.

[2] White, *The Desire of Ages*, p. 637.

[3] Philip Yancey, *Where Is God When It Hurts?* (Grand Rapids: Zondervan, 1977), p. 63.

[4] It should be recognized that the primary purpose of the authors of Eze. 28 and Isa. 14 was not to describe the fall and character of the pre-fallen Lucifer. The prophets were speaking of Israel's historical enemies. The supernatural, however, "appears by way of analogy." The biblical authors represent the quite human kings of Tyre and Babylon as having that selfishness and pride that stand at the very base of the sin problem. Thus the prophets liken them to Lucifer. See Alden Thompson, *Who's Afraid of the Old Testament God?* (Grand Rapids: Zondervan, 1989), pp. 56-58.

[5] For critiques of the strengths and weaknesses of Grotius's governmental theory of the atonement, see George Barker Stevens, *The Christian Doctrine of Salvation* (New York: Charles Scribners Sons, 1905), pp. 157-173; H. D. McDonald. *The Atonement of the Death of Christ* (Grand Rapids: Baker, 1985), pp. 203-207. For a positive exposition of the governmental theory from an Arminian perspective, see John Miley, *Systematic Theology* (New York: Eaton and Mains, 1892, 1894), vol. 2, pp. 155-202.

[6] Loraine Boettner, *Studies in Theology*, 5th ed. (Grand Rapids: Eerdmans, 1960), pp.

287, 286; cf. Anselm *Cur Deus Homo* 1. xii.

[7] White, *The Desire of Ages*, p. 761. (Italics supplied.)

[8] Anselm *Cur Deus Homo* 1. viii. (Italics supplied.)

[9] Peter Abelard's commentary on Romans 3:19-26, quoted in John R. W. Stott, *The Cross of Christ* (Downers Grove, Ill.: InterVarsity, 1986), p. 217.

[10] Stevens, *The Christian Doctrine of Salvation,* pp. 157-159.

[11] Robinson, *Redemption and Revelation*, p. 267.

[12] Vincent Taylor, *The Atonement in New Testament Teaching*, 2nd ed. (London: Epworth, 1945), p. 63.

[13] Karl Heim, *Jesus the World's Perfecter*, trans. D. H. van Daalen (Philadelphia: Muhlenberg, 1961), p. 101.

[14] Jürgen Moltmann, *The Crucified God*, trans. R. A. Wilson and John Bowden, 2nd ed. (New York: Harper & Row, 1973), p. 175.

[15] P. T. Forsyth, *The Cruciality of the Cross* (Wake Forest, N.C.: Chanticleer, 1983), p. 102.

[16] Ellen G. White, *Patriarchs and Prophets* (Mountain View, Calif.: Pacific Press, 1958), pp. 68, 69. (Italics supplied.)

[17] A. Graham Maxwell, *Can God Be Trusted?* (Nashville: Southern Pub. Assn., 1977), p. 41.

[18] H. E. Guillebaud, *Some Moral Difficulties of the Bible* (London: Inter-Varsity Fellowship, 1941), p. 18.

[19] Fritz, Guy, "The Universality of God's Love," in *The Grace of God, the Will of Man: A Case for Arminianism*, ed. Clark H. Pinnock (Grand Rapids: Zondervan, 1989), pp. 33-35.

[20] Alister E. McGrath, *The Mystery of the Cross* (Grand Rapids: Zondervan, 1988), p. 123.

[21] Ralph P. Martin, *Reconciliation: A Study of Paul's Theology*, rev. ed. (Grand Rapids: Zondervan, 1989), p. 57.

[22] White, *Patriarchs and Prophets*, pp. 41-43. (Italics supplied.) Cf. White, *The Desire of Ages*, p. 759.

[23] Albert C. Knudson, *The Doctrine of Redemption* (New York: Abingdon Cokesbury, 1933), p. 365; Leon Morris, *The Cross of Jesus* (Grand Rapids: Eerdmans, 1988), p. 9. (Italics supplied.)

[24] P. T. Forsyth, *The Justification of God* (London: Latimer House, 1948), pp. 98, 122. (Italics supplied.)

[25] C. S. Lewis, *The Four Loves* (New York: Harcourt Brace Jovanovich, 1960), p. 163.

[26] For discussions of God's holiness, see Emil Brunner, *The Christian Doctrine of God*, trans. Olive Wyon (Philadelphia: Westminster, 1949), pp. 157-174; G. R. Lewis, "God, Attributes of," in *Evangelical Dictionary of Theology*, ed. Walter A. Elwell, p. 455.

[27] Forsyth, *Cruciality of the Cross*, pp. 70, 71, 23; P. T. Forsyth, *Positive Preaching and the Modern Mind* (New York: George H. Doran, n.d.), p. 354.

Chapter 2

God's Problem With Me

The law of the tombstone is universal. It declares that there are enough to go around and that every person gets one sooner or later. For some of us the route to the grave is short, for others it is long, but for all it is certain, because "the wages of sin is death" (Rom. 6:23) and "all have sinned and fall short of the glory of God" (Rom. 3:23).

Perhaps God's most fateful act was in trusting His created beings with free will. That decision opened the way for rebellion against His rulership in both heaven and earth.

Free will provided human beings with the possibility of rejecting their creatureliness and their dependence upon God. Worse yet, it supplied the opportunity for people to declare their self-dependence, their autonomy—a fact evidenced daily in modern culture's sophisticated psychological and philosophical theories and in its artistic creations.

Defiant humanity proclaims its equality with God. Sin is the arrogant desire to be the god of our own lives. Thus all sin flows from disregard of the first great commandment: "You shall love the Lord your God with all your heart, and with all your soul, and with all your mind" (Matt. 22:37).

Sin and its results have touched the entire human race. Maybe you know someone who is not a sinner. I don't. Or perhaps you know someone not under the curse of death. I don't. If the most basic fact in the cosmic crisis of sin is that God is in trouble, the second most important fact, at least from the human perspective, is that humanity is also in difficulty. On every hand humans as individuals and as societies face what seem to be insurmountable problems.

This chapter will examine several of the deepest of those difficulties, since before we can understand the work of Christ for us in salvation, we must clearly see what we need to be saved from. But even before that examination, it is crucial to recognize that we cannot solve our own problems.

Fig Leaves and Swimming Pools

When I was a boy I used to have the same dream again and again. It always took place at the local swimming pool. Everyone always wore a swimsuit—everyone, that is, except me. I still remember the frightful vividness of that Technicolor, quadraphonic dream. It was one of the most uncomfortable experiences of my young life. In desperation I would run into the dressing room to cover my nakedness, only to find that the walls had disappeared. I could find no way to cover my shame. Relief came only when I awoke from my sweaty misery.

We read of a similar experience in the story of Adam and Eve found in Genesis 3. After they willed to become the god of their lives and to eat the forbidden fruit, the Bible says that "the eyes of both were opened, and they knew that they were naked" (verse 7). In that state they had a frightening sense that something was wrong. Having broken their connection with God, they now suffered the pangs of guilt. Unlike my imaginary nakedness, however, theirs was real. Their guilt was true guilt. They had sinned and were under the conviction of God's Holy Spirit.

In their desperation, the Bible says, "they sewed fig leaves together and made themselves aprons" (verse 8). Have you ever thought about the effectiveness of such garments?

Here is an experiment that many who live in warmer climates can try. During my childhood in northern California we had a huge fig tree in our backyard. In my mind's eye I often have viewed myself going out there, taking off all my clothes, and fashioning a garment from those leaves. No matter how hard I strain at my mental task, the results always turn out the same—ridiculous and ineffective. Such a garment is hardly something I would feel comfortable wearing to the local shopping mall.

The fig leaves in Genesis 3 represent Adam and Eve's attempt to cover their own nakedness. We can equate such attempts with salvation by works. Verse 21 reinforces the ineffectiveness of their human efforts at covering their spiritual nakedness, when it says that "the Lord God made for Adam and for his wife garments of skins, and clothed them"—an act of grace.

But even the skins of animals were not the real covering that God had in mind for human "nakedness." The only solution in the long run would be the acceptance of the robe of Revelation's Lamb (Rev. 3:18; 6:11; 7:9, 13, 14; Luke 15:22).

Chapter 3 will have more to say on the topic of animal skins and the Lamb's robe. The important thing to understand at this point is that human beings are totally incapable of covering their own nakedness—of solving the sin problem. That is evident from Adam's reaction to God's initial visit to Eden after the entrance of sin. We turn now to some of the major results of human sin.

Alienation and Estrangement

The first thing we notice about Adam and Eve after the entrance of sin is that they were uncomfortable in their sporty new fig-leaf outfits—so much so, in fact, that they "hid" from the God who had previously been their friend. Taking the initiative (an act of grace), He searched for the guilt-ridden pair, asking Adam what the problem was. The man replied that he had hid because of his nakedness (Gen. 3:8-10).

Thus an immediate result of sin was alienation or estrangement between individuals and God. Such alienation is quite understandable on the human plane. For example, children who have violated their mother's will do not wish to meet her, or to look her in the face. They have something in their heart that they wish to hide. Likewise, guilt renders God's presence unbearable. Sin ruptured the oneness between people and God.

The sin-caused alienation problem between God and the human race would have been bad enough if it had been only a passive hiding from God's presence, but sin by its very nature is active against Him. James claims that the natural world is at "enmity with God" (James 4:4). Another meaning for "enmity" is "hostility." And Paul tells us that God reached out to save us when we were His "enemies" (Rom. 5:10; Col. 1:21, 22).

"Now an enemy," Leon Morris notes, "is not simply someone who falls a little short of being a good and faithful friend. He belongs in the opposite camp." Sinners, by definition, "are putting their effort into the opposite direction to that of God."[1]

Sin, as we noted earlier, is active rebellion against God's government, His laws, and His person. It is a vigorous disposition to place my "self" and my will instead of God and His will at the center of my life. The scene of the macrocosmic struggle between good and evil in the universe replicates itself in the heart and mind of every individual. Each person's life is the scene of a death-grapple between good and evil. The result is a broken relationship between the Creator and the individual. You and I were born at enmity with God.

Alienation, unfortunately, is not merely a fact of life between people and God. F. W. Dillistone points out that it is "scarcely possible to take up any interpretation of the human situation . . . without soon encountering the concept of alienation."[2]

That conclusion is central to the story of Genesis 3. After God discovered the fig-leafed Adam and Eve cowering in the garden, He asked Adam how they had discovered that they were naked. More specifically, God inquired if they had eaten the forbidden fruit.

Adam replied that it wasn't really his fault. "The woman whom thou gavest to be with me, she gave me fruit of the tree, and I ate" (Gen. 3:12, KJV).

Now here is an interesting illustration of the immediate result of sin. I often ask my students how many perfect marriages they are aware of. The response divides itself somewhat down the middle—between the already marrieds and the not-yet marrieds.

A few in the latter group condescendingly smile, knowing that while all previous marriages have developed problems, their own soon-to-be-entered state of married bliss is destined to be different.

The former group knowingly smirk in remembrance of shattered illusions.

I generally remark that the only perfect marriages are those that have yet to be consummated. Perhaps for the future of the race it is fortunate that "love" tends to be both blind and naive.

At any rate, with Adam and Eve we have the first and only perfect marriage. Their lives were in harmony with each other and their goals were the same, each serving the other as a "helper." We must view the brutal alienation that developed immediately after the entrance of sin in that light. Whereas a short time before, the Edenic pair had lived in harmony, now Adam turns on Eve rather than confess his own fault. "It's not my fault, God. That woman gave it to me. She's the problem." Thus sin brought the first family argument. Husbands and wives have spent a great deal of time trying to pin blame on each other ever since. The stereotyped picture we have here is that of two "lovers" each pointing angrily at the other and shouting simultaneously, "It's your fault."

The problem that infects husbands and wives extends throughout all society. The atheistic Jean-Paul Sartre captured the biblical picture nicely. "Hell is . . . other people!" he exclaimed at the conclusion of *No Exit*, a play that pictures two women and a man trying to get along with each other in a room without windows or doors.[3]

Alienation in Genesis 3 does not stop with God and other people. It even affects a person's relationship with his or her own "self." After God left off questioning Adam, He moved to Eve. "What," He asked her, "is this that you have done?" "The devil made me do it," she replied (verse 13, paraphrased).

Here we come face to face with the human problem of people being both unwilling and, in most cases, unable to face up to themselves and to evaluate correctly their actions and their underlying motives.

Now, it is true that I don't mind confessing sin, but I would rather acknowledge your sin than mine. In fact, I can talk about yours for hours, receiving a kind of subtle satisfaction from the fact that you may be worse than I, or at least as bad.

Of course, I don't mind confessing those things that do not make much difference to me. But come close to my favorite sins, and I will give you a lively and evasive fight that may be as brutal as it is deceptive. Jeremiah hit the nail on the head when he noted that "the heart is deceitful above all things, and desperately corrupt" (Jer. 17:9). Thus a third great alienation that took place at the entrance of sin into the world was estrangement from our own selves. But even that is not the end of the separations brought about by sin.

A fourth alienation took place in humanity's relation to the world of nature. At Creation, God gave Adam and Eve "dominion" over the natural world. As His vice-regents over the earth, they were in harmony with the world around them. That relationship came to an abrupt halt at the Fall. God declared that henceforth the ground would be cursed because of their sin: "In toil you shall eat of it all the days of your life; thorns and thistles it shall bring forth to you" (Gen. 3:17, 18).

The truth of that statement is obvious to anyone who likes to garden. I plant one every year, and the thing that strikes me is that the weeds grow all by themselves, while I have to labor long and hard to get healthy corn and tomatoes. That situation constantly verifies God's word to Adam that he would earn his bread in the "sweat" of his face (verse 19). Where once harmony existed between people and nature, since the Fall the natural world has become an enemy to be conquered with great exertion and violence. That state of affairs is a perpetual reminder that humanity is at war with its Creator.

We can conclude then that an immediate result of sin was a series of relational breakdowns, the first being between individuals and God. Isaiah declared to Israel that "your iniquities have made a separation between you and your God; and your sins have hid his face from you so that he does not hear" (Isa. 59:2). God has a legitimate problem with the inhabitants of His rebel planet, and He cannot bless them as He would like.

Unfortunately, humanity's separation from its Maker has applied to all its relationships. Human beings live in a world of alienations that they are helpless to make right. The Cain and Abel story reveals that those of Genesis 3 did not end in that chapter. The continuing crisis looms large throughout Scripture.

War, divorce, mental illness, and ecological disaster are major themes of world history outside of the Bible. Our utopian dreams continue to fade into the distant future, and human helplessness in the face of history seems to proclaim that any reconciliation must come from outside the human sphere if it is to occur at all.

Slavery at Its Worst

A second fruit of humanity's warfare against God is servitude to His enemy. To understand the problem clearly, we need to take a look at the myth of human freedom that existential psychology so avidly propounds.

Fourteen years of my professional career I spent studying and teaching the philosophy of education. That job gave me the opportunity of exploring both the philosophy and the psychology of the autonomous individual—the person who makes decisions without external interference and then puts them into practice in the everyday world.

I learned a lot about the "natural goodness" of children. Working within the tradition of Jean-Jacques Rousseau and Sigmund Freud, many educational theories have developed in the twentieth century that imply that successful education is not something taught to children by adults. Rather, the secret of success is not to impose upon children from the outside, but to provide them with an atmosphere of total freedom so that their natural goodness can float to the top.[4]

Now, that is a beautiful theory. But just ask any elementary school teacher (or parent), and he or she will tell you that what floats to the top is not undiluted goodness. What the humanistic psychologists miss in their beautiful theories is the very real problem of sin in human nature.

The Bible teaches that humans have freedom of choice but that that freedom is not absolute in the sense that people are autonomous or totally free. Rather, biblical freedom exists in the sense that individuals can choose Jesus Christ as Lord and live by His principles, or elect Satan as master and make themselves subject to his laws.

Paul wrote to the believers in Rome that "you are slaves of the one whom you obey, either of sin, which leads to death, or of obedience, which leads to righteousness" (Rom. 6:16). Thus we have freedom to choose within bounds, but we do not have absolute freedom.

When Adam and Eve rebelled against the government and law of God, they placed themselves under the rulership of Satan and the principles of his kingdom. Whereas once they had a natural inclination toward goodness, now, Ellen White writes, "every" person has "a bent to evil, a force which, unaided, he cannot resist." She does not claim that people are totally evil all the time, but that they tend toward evil rather than goodness. While there remains "a desire for goodness" in every human heart, that desire must struggle against the downward bent of human nature.[5]

Sin is more than an outward act or a series of them. It is, John R. W. Stott explains, "a deep-seated inward corruption."[6] The Bible calls such a condition the earthly, fleshly, or unspiritual nature (2 Cor. 1:12; 1 Peter 2:11; 1 Cor. 2:14).

Because sin is an inward corruption of the heart and mind, it holds us in bondage. The daily life of the "natural person" is tainted and twisted with a self-centeredness that leads to unloving behavior toward both God and fellow humans.

The Bible repeatedly refers to people as being "slaves" to sin (e.g., John 8:34). The human race entered into that bondage when Adam sinned in Eden and became naked through losing the robe of sonship (Rom. 5:12; Gen. 3:7-10). Since Genesis 3 humanity has been under Satan's reign.

Slavery, by definition, implies helplessness. A slave is one who is *owned* by the master. Paul aptly described the servitude into which sin takes us when he wrote to Titus that Christians once had been "slaves to various passions and pleasures" (Titus 3:3).

Those doubting the depth of the slavery to sin need only recall their personal struggles with it. James highlights the difficulty by noting that any person who "makes no mistakes in what he says . . . is a perfect man" (James 3:2). After several illustrations regarding the depth of the problem, he writes that "every kind of beast and bird, of reptile and sea creature, can be tamed [controlled] and has been tamed by humankind, but no human being can tame the tongue" (verses 7, 8). One unguarded moment, and the tongue undoes all the effort that has gone into its discipline. The same applies to such problems as control of the temper or lustful thoughts. We struggle and struggle, only to slide back again.

Paul graphically described the bondage problem in Romans 7: "I find it to be a law that when I want to do right, evil lies close at hand. For I delight in the law of God, in my inmost self, but I see in my members another law at war with the law of my mind and making me *captive* to the law of sin which dwells in my members. Wretched man that I am! Who will deliver me from this body of death?" (verses 21-24).

The point is not that we never overcome some bad habit through heroic moral effort from time to time, but that we never come to the place where we break all our bad habits. As a result of my strenuous efforts I have had a victory over a besetting sin from time to time, but I have discovered that while I am using all my moral concentration in "holding down" temptations at one point, another opportunity to pamper myself and uplift my ego pops up behind me. Furthermore, no sooner do I overcome on one point than I become proud of the fact and thereby fall into the same pit from the opposite direction. *Bondage* and *slavery* are apt terms for such a condition.

A Dirtier Than Dirt Defilement

Some things are dirtier than others. I once stepped in something ultimately disgusting, especially since I was barefoot at the time. But a little soap and water took it off and not only made me feel clean but actually cleansed the problem. More serious was the occasion when I stained my hands picking green walnuts. No matter how long and how hard I scrubbed, the stains just wouldn't come off. Fortunately, time took care of the problem. Within a few weeks my hands were as good as new. But there is at least one sort of defilement that neither soap and water nor time is able to remove.

That thought brings us to a third consequence of the revolt against God—moral defilement. Down through history people have struggled with the nagging fear that they aren't clean, that something in their life is dirty. In fact, when people do something wrong they often claim that they feel "dirty."

Defilement and the need for cleansing stand at the center of much of the world's great literature. Nathaniel Hawthorne's *Scarlet Letter* provides us an example of both defilement and a felt need for cleansing. A pervasive sense of defilement has even shaped human language. Thus we speak of "dirty money," a "filthy joke," and "dirty politics."

Likewise, Christian hymnody has expressed what appears to be a universal problem with such phrases as "Wash me, and I shall be whiter than snow" and "washed in the blood of the lamb." Such language has its roots in Scripture. David, for example, writes: "Purge me with hyssop, and I shall be clean" (Ps. 51:7) and God through Isaiah counsels his readers to "wash" themselves and make themselves "clean" of moral impurity (Isa. 1:16). He goes on to promise that even "though your sins are like scarlet, they shall be as white as snow" (verse 18). The last book of the Bible expresses the same problem when it speaks of those who have "washed their robes and made them white in the blood of the Lamb" (Rev. 7:14).

William Johnsson sums up the issue when he notes that "man's basic problem is that he is dirty, defiled. Indeed, the *universal* need is for purgation" or cleansing.[7]

A More Powerful Bondage Than Sin

A third result of humanity's rebellion is death. The firmer and more permanent bondage of death, which Paul refers to as king (Rom. 5:17), eventually supersedes slavery to sin. Death is the terminal consequence of the rebellion that separated humanity from the source of life.

The reign of death flows right out of Genesis 3. God had told the race's parents that they would die "in the very day" that they ate the fruit (Gen. 2:17). Did they perish that day? Yes and no. Physically they lived on many years, but spiritually they died when they separated themselves from the source of life. Their death was primarily spiritual. Since the fall that has been the human race's natural condition. That is why Jesus calls the beginning of the Christian life a "new birth," or a birth from above (John 3:3, 5, 6). Eventually, however, death affected humanity's total being. The immediate results, however, were spiritual, with the physical following.

Death first transformed Adam's entire person, then all of humanity. "The conviction of the indissoluble connection between evil and wrong, between death and sin," Emil Brunner writes, "permeates the whole of the Bible."[8] "As sin came into the world through one man and death through sin," Paul penned, ". . . so death spread to all men because all men sinned" (Rom. 5:12). Again, he noted, "the wages of sin is death" (Rom. 6:23). The entire human race is legally under the death penalty.

At this point it is important to recognize that Adam's and Eve's deaths were partly the result of separation from the source of life and partly the result of God's penal action against them. Regarding the penal nature of their deaths, Genesis 3:22-24 indicates that God "drove" them out of Eden, lest they should continue to partake of the tree of life and live forever. It was far from being a mere natural result. God actively intervened in the course of history to ensure their deaths. His act was one of mercy, lest they infinitely extend the misery and woe of sin.

The Wrath of God

Thus far in our study we have examined the human troubles resulting from sin in terms of alienation, bondage to sin, death, and defilement. While such topics are not pleasant, they are much more so than the wrath of God.

God's wrath is one of the most unpopular phrases in many sectors of modern theology. "Nothing is commoner," James Denney wrote, "than the denial that the revelation of divine wrath is real. The wrath of God, it is constantly asserted, is an idea which is ultimately inconsistent with the Christian conception of God as a loving father."[9]

C. S. Lewis, writing in the same vein, suggests that what most people want is "not so much a Father in Heaven as a grandfather in heaven"—kind of a "senile benevolence."[10] Preferring to regard God as the father who unconditionally welcomes back the prodigal son, we don't like to think that we have anything to fear from Him. For many years I personally sought to play down and explain away the biblical teaching regarding God's wrath. It wasn't until I began to prepare for writing on the topic that I was forced to come to terms with the issue.

Even though the concept of wrath is quite unpopular with many theologians and lay Christians, it was extremely popular with God. The number of Bible references to His wrath exceeds 580. The Old Testament alone uses more than 20 words for the wrath of God. Divine wrath, therefore, was not an occasional topic.[11]

What apparently bothers most of us about God's wrath, J. I. Packer suggests, is that it seemingly implies something "*unworthy of God*," such as a bad temper, loss of self-control, or an irrational outburst.[12] That fear, given our human use of the term, is understandable, even if it is misleading.

But we must not confuse human wrath and divine wrath. God is not a person of weakness and uncontrollable anger. The "wrath of God," writes G. C. Berkouwer, "is not an irrational or an incomprehensible kind."[13] Unlike the unpredictable anger of a sinful human being, divine wrath is, and always has been, totally consistent and predictable. The pagans worshiped capricious gods, and their worshipers could not guess what their deities would do next. They were never sure when their gods would be angry and annoyed with them.

The ancient Hebrews, on the other hand, had no such difficulty in predicting the wrath of Yahweh. Only one thing aroused His wrath—*SIN*. They knew that God was always angry with sin. In the Old Testament idolatry particularly triggered divine wrath (Ex. 32:8-10). But such sins as adultery (Eze. 23:27), the mistreatment of widows and orphans (Ex. 22:22-24), covetousness and falsehood (Jer. 6:11-15), violence (Eze. 8:17, 18), sin in general (Job 21:20), and all other transgressions of His person and His law also provoked it.

The Cross of Christ

Contrary to the views of many, the God of the Old Testament did not with the coming of Jesus transform Himself into a "gentleman" who would henceforth dispense with all further recourse to wrath and judgment. The New Testament portrayal of God, and even of Christ, is one of both judgment and wrath. The words for "wrath" and "anger," for instance, appear 13 times in Revelation 6 through 19.[14] Particularly expressive, and even surprising to most readers, is the revelator's poignant phrase: "the wrath of the Lamb" (Rev. 6:16).

Of course, one might expect such teachings in the frightful book of Revelation. It is therefore significant that the great gospel book of Romans builds its salvational package on the inescapable problem of God's wrath. "For the wrath of God," Paul writes, "is revealed from heaven against all ungodliness and wickedness of men who by their wickedness suppress the truth" (Rom. 1:18). In chapter 2 Paul goes on to note that the impenitent are "storing up wrath" for "the day of wrath when God's righteous judgment will be revealed" (verse 5). "There will be wrath and fury," he adds, for those who "do not obey the truth, but obey wickedness" (verse 8).

The Gospel of John teaches that the wrath of God will rest upon any who reject Christ (John 3:36). In addition, Jesus frequently referred to the outworking of divine wrath (without using the word) in His explicit teachings on the reward of the wicked. For those who stayed in rebellion against God there would be "gnashing of teeth" and "the hell of fire" (Matt. 24:51, KJV; 5:22). "Do not," He cautioned, "fear those who kill the body but cannot kill the soul; rather fear him who can destroy both soul and body in hell" (Matt. 10:28).

It is impossible to take the Gospels seriously and yet maintain that Jesus did not teach the reality and fury of God's wrath. The Gospel writers even portray Jesus as having wrath during His ministry. For example, when the Pharisees were more concerned with their Sabbath rules than with the healing of a man's crippled hand, Mark writes that "he looked around at them with anger ['wrath' in Greek], grieved at their hardness of heart" (Mark 3:5). With this evidence, and much more, in hand, Gustav Stählin concludes that "wrath is an essential and inalienable trait in the biblical and NT view of God." The root causes for that wrath are the "disregard for the revelation of His being in creation (R[om]. 1:18, 21ff.) and also the disdaining and transgression of the revelation of His will in the Law (R[om]. 2:17ff.; 3:19f.)."[15]

God's wrath is not only a reaction against disregard for His personal holiness and the sacredness of His law, but a holy reaction to the woe and

God's Problem With Me

misery resulting from rebellion against His government—a rebellion that (as we saw earlier) brought alienation, slavery, death, and defilement in its train. Sin has brought untold suffering to the universe and to God's created beings.

"What," queried H. Wheeler Robinson, "will be the reaction of the holy God to the impact of this suffering?" Robinson goes on to suggest that the best way to answer his question would be to ask how a "good man" would react to the evil that he encounters in the world around him. "Surely he will feel and show uncompromising antagonism to it. Whatever allowances he may make for the history and circumstances of the evil-doer, . . . he will react with a righteous indignation and a justifiable wrath."[16]

The response of a holy God to sin and its sufferings will be infinitely stronger than that of "good men." Thus God's "wrath only goes forth because God is Love, and because sin is that which injures His children and is opposed to the purpose of His Love."[17]

God's wrath is not opposed to His love. Rather, it is an outgrowth of that very love. The more love, the more indignation at sin and its results, and thus the more wrath. The opposite of love is not wrath, but indifference.

Because God loves His creation, He cares what happens to it. Divine love, Richard Rice writes, is "deadly serious." "Because God loves us, everything about us matters to him. He therefore cannot ignore our sins. . . . It distresses him to see the ones he loves" destroyed. Being "utterly ruthless in the face of sin throughout the Bible," God "cannot stand idle while people he loves destroy themselves."[18]

Thus wrath is the natural fruit of divine love and not in opposition to it. Alan Richardson put it forcefully when he wrote that "only a certain kind of degenerate Protestant theology has attempted to contrast the wrath of God with the mercy of Christ."[19] God, as the Bible pictures Him, cannot and will not stand idly by while His creation suffers. *His reaction is judgment on sin, and we should see this judgment as the real meaning of biblical wrath.* God condemns sin in judgment and will eventually move to destroy it completely. He waits only for the entire universe to acknowledge that He is doing the right thing. Once sin fully matures so that all creation recognizes that God is right in His judgment on sin and sinners, He will react to annihilate both (Rev. 20:13-15; see also chapter 6 of this book).

Wrath, as we have seen, is a central teaching of both Testaments. A God without wrath would be a God who doesn't care about His creation. Furthermore, a God without wrath lacks both love and holiness. "To deny the wrath of God," H. D. McDonald asserts, "is to have . . . a God who has lost interest in the man he created for fellowship with himself and who has no concern to maintain his moral order in the world."[20]

God has wrath because He cares. Those who care less have less anger at sin. R. W. Dale perceptively noted that "it is partly because sin does not provoke our own wrath that we do not believe that sin provokes the wrath of God."[21]

While wrath is an integral part of the divine Personality, it fortunately "does not exhaust the activity of that Personality." God is more than Judge of all the earth—He is also its Redeemer.[22]

The good news is not that God is not wrathful, but that Christ bore the penalty of (God's judgment on) sin for all who believe in Him. Thus, Paul, speaking of Christ's blood, wrote that we shall be "saved by him from the wrath of God" (Rom. 5:9). In a similar manner, the Gospel of John claims that "he who believes in the Son has eternal life; he who does not obey the Son shall not see life, but the wrath of God rests upon him" (John 3:36). Again, Paul penned, "God has not destined us for wrath, but to obtain salvation through our Lord Jesus Christ, who died for us" (1 Thess. 5:9, 10). Christ tasted the cup of wrath for all humanity, but those who refuse His sacrifice will drink their own cup. "If a man does not repent," the Psalmist noted, "God will whet his sword; he has bent and strung his bow" (Ps. 7:12).

God's wrath is primarily an end-time (eschatological) experience.[23] Jesus will deliver His people from "the wrath to come" (1 Thess. 1:10). At the same time, however, the wrath of God has also been evident periodically in the course of history at crucial junctures as He has broken into that history when the forces of evil threatened to overwhelm the interests of His kingdom.

Closely related to the above issue is the nature of divine wrath—that is, whether it is a personal outworking of His "anger," or whether it is impersonal in the sense that the wrath of God is merely the natural consequence of sin. Many twentieth-century Christians have held the latter position. New Testament scholar C. H. Dodd, for example, wrote that the idea of an angry (wrathful) God is a concept "which breaks down as the rational element in religion advances." Divine wrath, he held, is an "impersonal," "inevitable process of cause and effect in a moral universe," rather than being a "feeling or attitude of God toward us." "Wrath is the effect of human sin." Having taken his cue from Paul's repeated use of "God gave them up" to such things as a base mind and dishonorable passions (Rom. 1:26, 28), Dodd noted that the wrathful "act of God is no more than an abstention from interference with their free choice and its consequences." Thus the wrath of God is basically passive.[24]

The concept of God's impersonal wrath does, it seems, have an element of truth in it. God does "give up" lawbreakers of physical and moral laws to the results of their actions. Thus habitual liars create distrust toward them, and sexual profligates risk the possibility of developing AIDS. Likewise, God lets the law of gravity take its effect on those who jump off tall buildings. Similarly, Yahweh permitted the Gentile nations to punish Israel when it overstepped its covenant bounds.

On the other hand, impersonal wrath does not exhaust the topic as far as Scripture is concerned. God certainly never just sat back in the case of Adam and Eve as natural consequences took their course. While such things played a part in an impersonal way, the personal aspect of God's wrath is also evident when the Bible says that God "drove" them out of Eden (Gen. 3:24). Similar events that indicate personal, active wrath on God's part in the Bible are the Noachian flood (Gen. 6:5-8); the earth's swallowing up of the rebellious families of Korah, Dathan, and Abiram (Num. 16:1-40); the development of leprosy on King Uzziah when he presumed to burn incense to the Lord in the sanctuary (2 Chron. 26:16-21); and the unnatural deaths of Ananias and Sapphira when they lied "to God" (Acts 5:1-11).

I suppose that we could view all these events as natural consequences, but that position seems to strain the imagination. Of course, a person could turn the idea of revelation on its head, as many critics have done, and explain away God's intervention by claiming that Scripture's stories are merely the biblical writers' rather superstitious explanations as to why Uzziah got leprosy, why Ananias and Sapphira died in close proximity to each other, and so on. But such an approach, if followed to its natural conclusions, essentially does away with any viable concept of divine revelation.

If seeking to make all divine wrath impersonal in history is difficult, it is next to impossible at the close of time. It appears to be quite personal to those who call for the mountains to fall on them to hide them from "the face of him who is seated on the throne, and from the wrath of the Lamb; for the great day of their wrath has come, and who can stand before it?" (Rev. 6:16, 17). The book of Revelation has much to say about God actively and personally breaking into history both to reward and punish individuals.

Brunner is most certainly correct when he claims that God's anger is as real as sin is real. He "reacts" against sin, Brunner writes, and "in the

Bible this divine reaction is called the wrath of God."[25] As Moses put it, God may be "slow to anger" (Ex. 34:6), but His anger is real and His wrath certain for those who refuse to halt their rebellion against His kingdom.

Perspective

In chapter 1 we examined the issues faced by God as a result of the sin problem. Chapter 2 looked at the consequences for humanity. The most important fact to note at present is that "the Bible reveals the astounding fact that in the face of our sin God keeps loving us."[26]

The next few chapters will examine the process by which God saves, heals, and restores repentant sinners to eternal life while still remaining just in the eyes of the universe. This work of atonement, McDonald writes, is "to bring about the reconciliation of God and man in a way consistent with the nature of God and the need of man."[27]

The process must protect the sanctity of God's law and moral government, and it must be in harmony with His holiness, justice, and love. Beyond that, God's plan must heal people's alienations, free the redeemed from slavery to sin, remove their death penalty, cleanse them from defilement, and save them from divine wrath. While the complexities of God's plan will challenge the greatest minds throughout the ceaseless ages of eternity, it is our privilege to begin to understand it in our present earthbound condition.

---

[1] Leon Morris, *The Atonement* (Downers Grove, Ill.: InterVarsity, 1983), pp. 136, 137.
[2] F. W. Dillistone, *The Christian Understanding of Atonement* (Philadelphia: Westminster, 1968), p. 399.
[3] Jean-Paul Sartre, *No Exit and Three Other Plays* (New York: Vintage, 1955), p. 47.
[4] See George R. Knight, *Philosophy and Education: An Introduction in Christian Perspective*, 4th ed. (Berrien Springs, Mich.: Andrews University Press, 2006), pp. 75-88, 104-114, 138, 139.
[5] Ellen G. White, *Education* (Mountain View, Calif.: Pacific Press, 1903), p. 29.
[6] John R. W. Stott, *Basic Christianity*, 2nd ed. (Downers Grove, Ill.: InterVarsity, 1971), p. 75.
[7] William G. Johnsson, *In Absolute Confidence: The Book of Hebrews Speaks to Our Day* (Nashville: Southern Pub. Assn., 1979), p. 101.
[8] Emil Brunner, *The Mediator*, trans. Olive Wyon (New York: Macmillan, 1934), pp. 479, 480.
[9] James Denney, *The Christian Doctrine of Reconciliation* (London: James Clarke, 1959), p. 144.
[10] C. S. Lewis, *The Problem of Pain* (New York: Macmillan, 1962), p. 40.
[11] Morris, *The Atonement*, p. 153.
[12] J. I. Packer, *Knowing God* (London: Hodder and Stoughton, 1973), pp. 134-136.

[13] G. C. Berkouwer, *Sin* (Grand Rapids: Eerdmans, 1971), p. 359.

[14] Robert H. Mounce, *The Book of Revelation*, New International Commentary on the New Testament (Grand Rapids: Eerdmans, 1977), pp. 347-349.

[15] Gustav Stählin, "The Wrath of Man and the Wrath of God in the NT," in *Theological Dictionary of the New Testament*, ed. G. Kittel and G. Friedrich, vol. 5, pp. 423, 441.

[16] Robinson, *Redemption and Revelation*, p. 268.

[17] W. L. Walker, *What About the New Theology?* 2nd ed. (Edinburgh: T. & T. Clark, 1907), pp. 148, 149. Cf. W. L. Walker, *The Gospel of Reconciliation or At-one-ment* (Edinburgh: T. & T. Clark, 1909), pp. 169, 170.

[18] Richard Rice, *The Reign of God* (Berrien Springs, Mich.: Andrews University Press, 1985), pp. 62, 176.

[19] Alan Richardson, *An Introduction to the Theology of the New Testament* (New York: Harper and Row, 1958), p. 77.

[20] McDonald, *Atonement of the Death of Christ*, p. 84.

[21] R. W. Dale, *The Atonement*, 14th ed. (London: Congregational Union of England and Wales, 1892), pp. 338, 339.

[22] Robinson, *Redemption and Revelation*, pp. 269, 270.

[23] See Raoul Dederen, "Atoning Aspects in Christ's Death," in *The Sanctuary and the Atonement*, ed. Arnold V. Wallenkampf and W. Richard Lesher (Washington, D.C.: [Biblical Research Committee of the General Conference of Seventh-day Adventists], 1981), p. 318; Denney, *Christian Doctrine of Reconciliation*, p. 146.

[24] C. H. Dodd, *The Epistle to the Romans* (London: Collins, Fontana Books, 1959), pp. 50, 49, 55. Cf. William E. Wilson, *The Problem of the Cross* (London: James Clarke, [c. 1929]), pp. 223, 224; Maxwell, *Can God Be Trusted?* pp. 82-84.

[25] Brunner, *The Mediator*, pp. 519, 518.

[26] Morris, *Cross of Jesus*, p. 4. Cf. White, *The Desire of Ages*, p. 37.

[27] McDonald, *Atonement of the Death of Christ*, p. 46.

Chapter 3

The Bible's Most Disgusting Teaching

It was 1:30 in the afternoon of June 4, 2007. I had just arrived home from an inspiring church service—so inspiring, in fact, that it led me to do strange things. Fortunately, my wife was at her sister's for the week.

After a quick microwaved lunch, I went out to the garage to get Scottie, our vibrant little cockapoo. As usual, his compliant little body responded to my call. Trustingly he looked up at me, hoping, no doubt, that I had a dog biscuit or two behind my back. I had something behind my back, all right, but it wasn't the kind of treat he was lusting after.

Picking up Scottie gently, I took him into the basement, since what I was about to do was not something I wanted the neighbors to be aware of. Safely secluded, I let the dog lie by my side as I set up my apparatus and knelt in prayer.

Then, placing my right hand on his head, I confessed my sins. Meanwhile, my left hand ran a well-honed knife across Scottie's unsuspecting and trusting throat. It was all over by 1:50.

The experience devastated me. I hadn't killed anything at all for years, let alone with my bare hands. As I knelt in a semi-stupor, I could feel the dying dog's arteries pulsating out his remaining blood—every throb thundering in my ears the message that "the wages of sin is death, the wages of sin is death." Nauseated almost beyond description, I stumbled over to the washbasin, where I sought to cleanse my sticky hands from the reminder that innocent little Scottie had died for my sins.

I felt bad about the dog, and I wasn't sure how I could ever explain it to my wife, but lambs aren't real plentiful in my part of Oregon.

The above experience was not inspired by the increasingly popular animal sacrifices of neo-witchcraft. Rather, I got the idea from the Bible. I wanted to catch the vividness of what the Old Testament sacrificial service must have meant to Adam and Eve and to those subsequent Israelites who maintained sensitivity to the meaning of the sacrificial system.

At this point, *I hope you realize that the above story is completely fictitious.* The reason I invented it was to bring the idea of substitutionary sacrifice a bit closer to home to a generation of readers for whom the killing of an animal with their hands (or by any other means) is a relatively meaningless experience that they once read about in the book of Leviticus. *If the illustration disgusted you, I have achieved my purpose*—a purpose aimed at highlighting the costliness of sin and its ugly consequences in Christ's life. My aim was to get readers to begin to grasp the realities reflected from Calvary, rather than to think of the cross merely on the level of imaginative platitudes that remove the brutality from sin and its results.

The Old Testament Foundation

The sacrificial service was probably meaningless for most ancient Israelites, since it soon became a repetitive ritual for the majority of its participants. Of one thing, however, we can be certain. Sacrifice must have been a mind-boggling personal experience for earth's first parents, individuals who had never seen anything dead before the entrance of sin.

Genesis 3:21 raises an intriguing idea when it notes that "the Lord God made for Adam and for his wife garments of skins, and clothed them." We last glimpsed Adam and Eve uncomfortably wearing their fig leaves. Now they have new clothes. Where, one is forced to ask, did these skins come from in a land populated by vegetarians (Gen. 1:29; 3:18)?

Although even conservative scholars hold that "it is unduly subtle . . . to foresee the atonement here,"[1] there seems to be fairly good contextual evidence that Adam and Eve had received instruction in the principles of substitutionary sacrifice at the time of the Fall. That possibility helps us make sense out of the Cain and Abel story in Genesis 4 and gives it significance.

As noted in chapter 1, I had a difficult time with Genesis 4 when I first read the Bible, because it seemed to me that Cain's offering was at least as good as Abel's. I even reasoned that Cain's offering was better than Abel's because it took more human effort (work) to raise fruit than it did to sit on a rock while the sheep ate and multiplied their numbers. That made it all the worse for me when God chose Abel's blood offering and "had no regard" for the good works of Cain. I found myself sympathizing with Cain and sharing his anger at such an injustice (verses 1-6). And I had no idea what God meant when He told Cain that if he did well, he would be accepted.

That story is senseless outside of a knowledge of substitutionary sacrifice. It wasn't until later that I came across Hebrews 11:4, which states that "by faith Abel offered to God a more acceptable sacrifice than Cain, through which he received approval as righteous, God bearing witness by accepting his gifts." By that time also I was coming to grips with the truths that "without the shedding of blood there is no forgiveness of sins" (Heb. 9:22) and that Christ was viewed by the New Testament writers as "the Lamb of God, who takes away the sin of the world" (John 1:29). In my maturer years I could see that Cain knew what I had not known when I first read the Bible.

In order to make sense out of his story, we need to see Cain's offering as disobedient rebellion (sin) in the face of instruction concerning the nature of sacrifice for sin and the symbolism involved in animal sacrifice. While some may argue that I have projected subsequent Old and New Testament ideas back into Genesis 4, the alternative is to read ignorance of the symbolism out of the scriptural silence concerning nearly every aspect of the lives of the earliest human beings. Such a course would make a potentially meaningful story into little more than an interesting bit of nonsense.

Ellen White suggests that our first parents and their children were not only "acquainted with the provision made for the salvation of man," but that they "understood the system of offerings which God had ordained." "The sacrificial offerings were ordained by God to be to man a perpetual reminder and a penitential acknowledgment of his sin and a confession of his faith in the promised Redeemer. They were intended to impress upon the fallen race the solemn truth that it was sin that caused death."[2]

A person can only imagine the impact of the sacrificial system on Adam and Eve, who had never seen anything die, let alone been the agent to take life. The fact that the wages of sin is death must have hit them with a force that subsequent earthlings, conditioned as we are to the "deadly" results of sin, can never comprehend. Certainly, as Adam performed that first sacrifice, it was clear to him that the animal had died for his personal sin.

Substitutionary sacrifice stands at the foundation of the symbols of salvation from the very beginning of post-Fall scriptural history. What the Bible implies through the experience of Adam and Eve became progressively more explicit as the Old and New Testament writers continued to add new bits and pieces to the puzzle of God's solution to the sin problem. And what was a somewhat irregular program of sacrifices for the early patriarchs became systematic in the time of Moses. The daily sacrifices and the important ritual on the day of atonement, which foreshadowed the great judgment of all sin, became a regular part of Hebrew life through the laws that God gave through Moses.

Interestingly enough, however, none of the Old Testament writers ever made explicit the meaning of the sacrifices. Vincent Taylor points out that "nowhere in the Old Testament is the rationale of sacrifice explained. The institution is taken for granted as a divine ordinance, and the only principle laid down is that 'the blood is the life.'"[3] As it was in Genesis 3 and 4, the meaning of the sacrifices must have been largely self-evident to those who performed them. Fortunately, particularly as it relates to the death of Christ, the New Testament is more explicit than the Old on the symbolism of substitutionary sacrifice.

On the other hand, as H. Wheeler Robinson notes, we can learn a great deal about the significance of Christ's death from the Old Testament, since New Testament usage had been "conditioned by the Old Testament meaning of sacrifice."[4] The sacrificial system was at the very heart of Israel's religious beliefs. When offered with the right intention, the sacrifices instituted approaches to God that signaled a new relationship to Him for both groups and individuals.

The Old Testament sacrificial system was essentially a substitutionary system. Sin had erected barriers between people and God. Beyond that, it meant death (Eze. 18:4). Sinners, bringing their sacrificial animals before the Lord, laid their hands on the animals' heads and confessed their sins, thereby symbolically transferring them to the animals that were to die as offerings (Lev. 1:4; 4:29; 16:21).[5] Thus, Gordon Wenham proposes, sacrifice removed the barrier of God's displeasure from between Him and the offender, thereby restoring fellowship and averting wrath.[6]

The clearest Old Testament text on the meaning of the sacrificial service is Leviticus 17:11: "For the life of a creature is in the blood, and I have given it to you to make atonement for yourselves on the altar; it is the blood that makes atonement for one's life" (NIV).

John Stott notes that the text makes three affirmations about the blood. First, blood is a symbol of life. Second, it makes atonement, in that the life of the innocent victim was given for the life of the sinful offerer. And third, God Himself offered the blood for the atonement. "I," God announces, "have given it to you to make atonement for yourselves." Thus even in the Old Testament, the sacrificial system was not a human device to placate God, but was provided by God Himself.[7]

Commenting on this passage, P. T. Forsyth points out that "the sacrifice is the result of God's grace and not its cause. It is given *by* God before

The Cross of Christ

it is given *to* Him. The real ground of any atonement is not in God's wrath but God's grace."[8]

Even in the Old Testament, therefore, it is God's initiative in grace that opens the way for atonement—for the barrier between humans and God erected by sin to be removed so that people can be at-one again with their Maker.[9]

The sacrificial system was a powerful object lesson on both the results of sin and the cost of its remedy for those who remained sensitive to its meaning. To men and women living in the ancient world, J. S. Whale writes, "sacrifice was no figure of speech but stark fact. . . . It asserted the powerful religious efficacy of shed blood." To modern people, however, it is a revolting idea on several grounds. Most twentieth-century people find the averting of "the divine displeasure by dashing the blood of an innocent victim against an altar, and sending the smoke from its burning flesh in clouds to heaven," to be "both morally and aesthetically disgusting."[10] With the accompanying flies, stench, and other sacrificial by-products, it must have been a messy business.

While Old Testament sacrifices may seem revolting, that of the New Testament, if you stop to think about it, is infinitely more distasteful and disgusting. The Old Testament sacrifices were only mere shadows pointing to the most incredible of all religious images: "the crucified God."[11]

The Crucified God

Sacrifice stands at the center of the language used by New Testament writers to describe the significance of Christ's death and the meaning of the gospel. The language and imagery of the Jewish system permeate New Testament discussions. Thus John the Baptist calls Jesus "the Lamb of God, who takes away the sin of the world" (John 1:29); Paul refers to Christ as "our paschal [Passover] lamb, [who] has been sacrificed" (1 Cor. 5:7); and Peter claims that his readers were not ransomed "with perishable things such as silver or gold, but with the precious blood of Christ, like that of a lamb without blemish or spot" (1 Peter 1:18, 19).

However, it is the book of Hebrews, with its extended comparison of Christ's work with the Jewish sacrificial system, that most clearly sets forth the idea that His death was a sacrifice for human sin. "Without the shedding of blood," the author of Hebrews claims, "there is no forgiveness of sins. Thus it was necessary for the copies of the heavenly things to be purified with these rites [the Jewish sacrificial system], but the heavenly things themselves with better sacrifices than these" (Heb. 9:22, 23). Christ "appeared once for all at the end of the age to put away sin by the sacrifice of himself" (verse 26). While "it is impossible that the blood of bulls and goats should take away sins," "Christ . . . offered for all time a single sacrifice for sins" (Heb. 10:4, 12).

What Christ accomplished in His life, death, and post-resurrection ministry had earlier provided an anticipatory "pattern" for the Levitical system (Heb. 8:1-7). We must therefore interpret, John Murray has perceptively noted, "the sacrifice of Christ in terms of the Levitical patterns because they were themselves patterned after Christ's offering."[12] Thus we find no separation between the imagery of the two Testaments. That of the New is, in fact, the fuller revelation of the meaning of the Old.

Beyond the continuity of sacrificial imagery between the Testaments, it also seems safe to say that if we would understand the cross we must see how Jesus regarded His mission. Perhaps His clearest statement on the topic of His death being a sacrificial offering took place during the Last Supper. "This is my blood of the covenant," He told the disciples, "which is poured out for many for the forgiveness of sins" (Matt. 26:28; cf. Mark 14:24).

The Gospel writers picture Jesus as being especially concerned with His death. For example, about halfway through his Gospel Mark has Jesus announcing that He must suffer many things, be rejected by the Jewish leaders, "and be killed, and after three days rise again" (Mark 8:31, 32; cf. Matt. 16:21). Jesus closely related that pronouncement with one requesting the disciples to take up their own crosses (Mark 8:34; Matt. 16:24). Mark records Jesus presenting His death two more times to His followers (Mark 9:30-32; 10:32-34). All the Gospel writers have Jesus completely identifying the purpose of His life with His suffering and death.

John, taking a somewhat different approach than the Synoptic Gospels, has Jesus moving toward the "hour" for which He had come into the world. His "hour" came on the evening before His death (John 12:27; 13:1). It began at the time of the Last Supper, ran through His Gethsemane experience, and climaxed on the cross.

All four Gospels have Christ's death, rather than His life or even His teachings, as their focal point. The Gospels are "abnormal biographies" in the sense that they give a disproportionate amount of space to the story of Christ's last few days on earth, His death, and His resurrection. Most biographies of great people take a quite different approach. A "normal" biography might have several hundred pages on the life and contributions of its subject, but only five to 10 pages on that person's death. That is because the biographer is primarily concerned with the individual's life.

The Cross of Christ

The Gospels may be unique in the history of world literature in this regard. Their focal point is the death of their hero, John even giving half his book over to the topic. Stranger yet, the Gospels do not have Jesus meeting a hero's death. To outward appearance, He perished in a Godforsaken death (Mark 15:34), because, as we learn from the New Testament authors, He was bearing the sins of the world and dying for the sins of all humanity. We will have a great deal more to say on the significance of the "Godforsakenness" of Jesus' death and His struggle in Gethsemane in chapter 5. At this juncture, however, it is sufficient to recognize that "death was not an incident in his [Christ's] life, as it is for us. It was his aim; it was the purpose and the climax of his messianic vocation."[13]

In spite of the forceful teachings of both the Old and New Testaments, a large segment of Christian scholars reject the sacrificial aspect of Christ's death. For example, after discounting Jesus' plain statement in Matthew 26:28 that flatly contradicts his opinion, Hastings Rashdall concluded in an influential book that "there is nothing in any of the narratives to suggest that the approaching death was in any way whatever to bring about the forgiveness of sins, or that Jesus was dying 'for' His followers in any other sense than that in which He had lived for them—in any sense but that in which other martyrs have died for their cause and for their followers." Rashdall went on to say that "there is nothing in the sayings attributed to the Master at the Last Supper which implies any fundamental difference in kind between the service which He was conscious of performing and the service to which He was inviting His disciples."[14]

Other scholars have postulated that the real model for the meaning of the plan of salvation is not sacrifice, but "the parable of the prodigal son who repents and is received by the father without the need for any elaborate machinery of reconciliation."[15] In this picture it is not God's judgment of sin that needs to be seen in the death of Christ, but rather that by His death He provided a living example of the Father's care. Jesus did not die as a sacrifice for sin, but because bad human beings reacted against His good teachings. Despite the opposition, Jesus kept proclaiming them. The result was martyrdom on the cross. "In this view of the atonement," William Wilson claims, "Christ's death has not the immediate and necessary connection with man's salvation which it had in tradition."[16]

In such a perspective it follows that Christ's teachings, example, and ability to inspire His followers to love God and to do good are more important than His death in the plan of salvation. Thus Horace Bushnell wrote that "atonement . . . is a change wrought in us."[17] In a similar vein,

The Bible's Most Disgusting Teaching

Robert Franks penned that "the problem of the Atonement is just that of bringing the sinner truly to acknowledge and confess his sin, and to turn in trustful obedience to the Father."[18]

The theory that Christ died to win us over to God's love and to inspire us to live our lives after the pattern of His life, as we shall see in chapter 7, has a great deal of truth in it, but taken as the primary reason for Christ's death, it dismisses the great bulk of Bible evidence claiming that Jesus bore our sins and died our death so that we might be "redeemed . . . from the curse of the law" (Gal. 3:13) with its death penalty (Rom. 6:23).

The idea that Jesus died to be a strong moral influence in favor of our loving God and living in obedience, claims Leslie Weatherhead, "goes a long way, but it does not go far enough. It doesn't go as far as the New Testament language takes us."[19] James Denney makes a valuable point when he remarks that "one can hardly help wondering whether those who tell us so confidently that there is no Atonement [sacrifice] in the parable of the prodigal have ever noticed that there is no Christ in it either—no elder brother who goes out to seek and to save the lost son, and to give his life a ransom for him."[20]

It seems safe to conclude that any biblical interpretation of Christ's death must take all the Bible evidence into consideration. We cannot merely select those aspects that harmonize with our rationalistic presuppositions.

Since the eighteenth-century Enlightenment, much of the violent reaction to Christ's death as a sacrifice for sin has resulted from extreme positions set forth in the post-Reformation era, concepts that suggested that Christ's death somehow "bought" God's favor and thereby changed His attitude toward sinners from one of opposition to one of love.

While such a reaction to a distorted teaching is understandable, the better part of wisdom is not to go to the other extreme by throwing out Christ's sacrificial death as a crucial feature in diverting God's judgment on sin from sinners to Himself (a topic discussed in chapter 4). Whether we like it or not, Emil Brunner suggests, "this alien element *is* the witness of the Primitive Christian Church. We can only get rid of it at the price of cutting ourselves off at the same time from the clear witness of the New Testament."[21]

Benjamin Warfield is even more forthright when he asserts that those who do not hold to the biblical view of Christ's sacrifice are not of "the same religion as the Christianity of the cross."[22]

For Paul the problem of the crucified God was the central feature of the gospel. "We preach Christ crucified," he wrote, "a stumbling block to Jews and folly to Gentiles, but to those who are called, . . . Christ [is] the power . . . and the wisdom of God" (1 Cor. 1:23, 24).

The Problem of the Innocent Suffering for the Guilty

Closely related to the argument over Christ's death as a "sacrifice" for sin is the issue of the innocent suffering for the guilty (that is, the substitutionary death of Christ).

In chapter 1 we noted the time-worn objections to the idea of substitution. "What man," asked Anselm in the eleventh century, "would not be judged worthy of condemnation if he were to condemn the innocent in order to let the guilty go free?" In a similar manner, Abelard wrote: "How cruel and wicked it seems that anyone should demand the blood of an innocent person as the price for anything, or that it should in any way please him that an innocent man should be slain—still less that God should consider the death of his Son so agreeable that by it he should be reconciled to the whole world!"[23]

In more recent times, John Macquarrie has labeled as "sub-Christian" the thought that "Christ was punished by the Father for the sins of men and in the place of men."[24] After all, argues William Newton Clarke in the first liberal systematic theology published in America, "punishment is absolutely untransferable, and no one can possibly be punished for the sin of another. . . . From its very nature, punishment can fall upon the sinner-alone."[25]

And hadn't Ezekiel written that "the soul that sins shall die"—that "the son shall not suffer for the iniquity of the father" and vice versa? "The righteousness of the righteous shall be upon himself, and the wickedness of the wicked shall be upon himself" (Eze. 18:20).

In the face of those statements and questions, however, the plain teaching of both the Old and New Testaments suggests the opposite conclusion. While "substitution" is not a biblical word, the concept was omnipresent in the Levitical sacrificial system. As we noted in the previous section and as Hans LaRondelle has succinctly summarized, "the idea that guilt can be transferred was the underlying principle of all Israel's symbolic sanctuary ritual; culminating in the annual scapegoat ceremony."[26]

Beyond that, James Stalker suggests, the New Testament doctrine of atonement has "its roots in the Old Testament; and without an appreciative knowledge of the sacrificial system of the old dispensation it can never be understood."[27]

The Bible's Most Disgusting Teaching

Thus Paul can define "the gospel" by saying that "Christ died for our sins," was buried, and rose on the third day (1 Cor. 15:1-3). Getting even more specific, the apostle wrote that Christ "was put to death for our trespasses and raised for our justification" (Rom. 4:25); "one has died for all. . . . For our sake he [God] made him [Jesus] to be sin who knew no sin, so that in him we might become the righteousness of God" (2 Cor. 5:14-21); "Christ redeemed us from the curse of the law, having become a curse for us—for it is written, 'Cursed be every one who hangs on a tree' " (Gal. 3:13). Basing his argument in Galatians 3 on Deuteronomy 21:23 and 27:26 (cf. Gal. 3:10), Paul argued that even though we, as law breakers, deserve to be excluded from God's covenant community, Christ took our place and assumed our penalty by becoming "a curse for us."

Other New Testament writers are just as clear on the topic. Peter, for example, penned that "he himself bore our sins in his body on the tree. . . . By his wounds you have been healed" (1 Peter 2:24). "Christ also died for sins once for all, the righteous for the unrighteous" (1 Peter 3:18; cf. Luke 22:37; Isa. 53:5, 6, 8, 11, 12).

That "Christ died for our sins" (1 Cor. 15:3) is foundational to the biblical doctrine of salvation. "He is our Saviour," J. Gresham Machen wrote, "not because He has inspired us to live the same kind of life that He lived, but because He took upon Himself the dreadful guilt of our sins and bore it instead of us on the cross."[28]

Martin Luther's Reformation theology rested in part upon the concept of substitutionary sacrifice. Writing to a monk in distress about his sins, Luther admonished: "Learn to know Christ and him crucified. Learn to pray to him and, despairing of yourself, say: 'Thou, Lord Jesus, art my righteousness, but I am thy sin. Thou hast taken upon thyself what is mine and hast given to me what is thine. Thou hast taken upon thyself what thou wast not and hast given to me what I was not.' " Luther referred to this as the "wonderful exchange."[29]

Ellen White had the same viewpoint when she penned that "Christ was treated as we deserve, that we might be treated as He deserves. He was condemned for our sins, in which He had no share, that we might be justified by His righteousness, in which we had no share. He suffered the death which was ours, that we might receive the life which was His."[30]

Even though substitution is a biblical concept, like many other Bible truths it is easily misunderstood. Any viable concept of substitution must be true to other biblical teachings. We must therefore separate it from all aspects of vindictiveness on God's part and from all legalistic approaches to heavenly bookkeeping that seek to equate so much suffering on Christ's part with so much quantitative sin on the part of humanity.

According to *Steps to Christ*, Jesus took upon Himself the guilt and the legal liabilities of our sin,[31] but He did not have our moral qualities transferred to Him. Although He took the penalty of sin upon Himself, we should not see the cross as vindictive punishment. Rather, we must view it as God's judgment on *sin*. "God," writes P. T. Forsyth, "made Christ sin in the sense . . . that God[,] as it were[,] took Him in the place of sin, rather than . . . the sinner, and judged the sin upon Him."[32]

At the very heart of substitution is the thought that Christ in His death did something that we could not do for ourselves. He paid the price that we could not, and "He saves us from dying in our sins."[33]

As we noted at the beginning of this section, certain thinkers down through history have held the idea of substitutionary sacrifice to be inherently immoral. They argue that neither sin nor righteousness can be transferred. Also at issue is the legal point that civil law may permit substitution, but criminal law does not.[34] For example, I may pay my best friend's speeding fine, but I may not take his place in jail for committing armed robbery or murder.

It seems that a basic problem here involves confusing human crime with sin. Michael Green points out an important distinction between crime and sin. We commit crimes against society, while sin is committed against a person (ultimately against God, the Creator of all people; see Ps. 51:4). It is beyond the prerogative of a judge to forgive a murderer, but the realm of personal relationships stands on a different basis. Sin has primarily to do with personal relationships, and individuals, including God, may freely forgive those they choose to forgive.[35]

Thus removing sin from the realm of crime to that of personal relationships eliminates some of the questionable aspects of substitution, but certainly not all of them. Why, for example, if God is an all-loving and all-powerful person, did Jesus need to die in order for the Father to be able to forgive?

- **Why Couldn't God Forgive Without the Death of Jesus on the Cross?**

In such texts as Matthew 6:14 and 18:33, 34, God has commanded us to forgive our neighbor unconditionally. He never suggested that our neighbor must make a sacrifice to atone for a wrong against us. We are merely told to forgive. Why, one might ask, doesn't God swallow His own

The Bible's Most Disgusting Teaching

medicine? Why doesn't He live by His own advice? Certainly God is powerful enough and loving enough to save all humanity with a wave of His hand. Why, then, did He send Christ?

Part of the answer, Anselm suggested, relates to who God is and the seriousness of sin.[36] While God is a private person, He is more than that—He is the Ruler of the universe. His problem, as we noted in chapters 1 and 2, is that a sector of His universe is in rebellion and that Satan has sown distrust of Him in the hearts of both the human and angelic rebels. God must solve the sin problem in a way that both expresses His love and upholds the laws of His kingdom. As a private person He could easily just forgive, but as Cosmic Ruler God must provide for stability. If He were to go out and extend forgiveness without putting into effect the penalty for the broken law of His kingdom, Satan would surely claim that God had lied. "See," he could say to his sympathizers, "sin doesn't result in death. God's word can't be trusted."

Given the nature of the challenge against Him, God had to devise a plan that would maintain His holy righteousness while, at the same time, allowing Him to forgive the guilty. Paul Tillich put the problem nicely when he wrote that "love becomes weakness and sentimentality if it does not include justice."[37]

Justice must be satisfied. To merely cancel it out by love would destroy the moral basis of the universe. Such a course would proclaim to all that God really didn't take His own laws and His own word seriously. "If sinners are to be saved," Leon Morris writes, "the fact of that broken law must be taken into consideration. It is the witness of the New Testament that Christ saves us in a way that does take that law into consideration."[38]

For God to forgive sin, it must be judged and condemned and its penalty nullified. "How then," John Stott queries, "could God express simultaneously his holiness in judgment and his love in pardon? Only by providing a divine substitute for the sinner, so that the substitute would receive the judgment and the sinner the pardon."[39]

Only by the greatness of the sacrifice can we measure the magnitude of human guilt. "Justice demands," Ellen White wrote, "that sin be not merely pardoned, but [that] the death penalty must be executed. God, in the gift of His only-begotten Son, met both these requirements. By dying in man's stead, Christ exhausted the penalty and provided a pardon."[40] Christ can forgive because He bore our sin.

"The cross," Brunner noted, "is the only possible way in which the absolute holiness and the absolute mercy of God are revealed together."[41] Thus

55

the cross of Christ "put God's forgiveness on a moral foundation,"[42] since the Divine Lawgiver and Divine Forgiver was also the Divine Victim.

Although many aspects of Christ's work remain obscure, one of the most pervasive concepts in both the Old and New Testaments, as evidenced in the first sections of this chapter, is that of substitutionary sacrifice. The very intricacy of sin, however, and the very complexity of God's love as expressed in the plan of salvation are beyond the reach of the human intellect. It is significant that God never even tried to make a full explanation in Scripture. *His answer was one of demonstration and revelation rather than complete explanation.* Substitution, claims Friedrich Büchsel, is a part of God's demonstration. "Revelation and substitution," he writes, "are not antithetical. Revelation comes to men only as substitution is made. God in His righteousness reveals more than a patience which leaves sin unpunished [Rom. 3] v. 26. He also reveals a holiness which is at one and the same time both grace and judgment."[43]

The most complete portrayal of God's love and justice and, on the other hand, the maliciousness of Satan's kingdom, came to a head at the cross of Calvary. There the perfect Lawkeeper was put to death by His enemy before the eyes of an onlooking universe. Christ, the fullest revelation of God (Heb. 1:1, 2), displayed both God's love and His justice. In the long run, as we shall see more fully in chapters 5 and 6, God's demonstration in Christ will put to rest lingering questions regarding the morality of substitutionary sacrifice. Meanwhile, we are left with the revelation of that event in the Bible.

The Unlovable Cross

The cross of Christ is the central symbol of Christianity, yet it would be hard to imagine a more disgusting image. For those of us who live in the twenty-first century, a cross can be a thing of beauty used to ornament our churches, our Bibles, or even our bodies, but it was never a thing of beauty or comfort in the first century of the Christian Era.

Rather, it was a cruel form of capital punishment. Even more than that, it was a device of political terror used to subjugate restless populations. It combined public shame with slow physical torture. The public shame consisted of dragging the cross (or at least its traverse beam) through the streets to the place of public execution. In an era that lacked TV programs and movies to satiate the downward bent of human desire toward violence, crucifixions were often the "best show" around for the bored and curious. Soldiers stripped offenders of all clothing and affixed the prisoners to the cross. The victims could not care for their bodily needs or hide their nakedness from the taunts and indignities of the spectators.

The physical tortures of crucifixion ranged from the nails driven through hands (or wrists) and feet to the inescapable burning of the Palestinian sun. The victim was immobile, therefore unable to fend off heat, cold, or insects. Death from fatigue, cramped muscles, hunger, or thirst usually came slowly, often after many days.

Roman law reserved crucifixion for the punishment of slaves and foreigners considered to be criminals. The authorities often used it for escaped slaves and rebels against the empire. The religious leaders condemned Jesus before Pilate as a political rebel.[44]

"The cross," Jürgen Moltmann writes, "is the really irreligious thing in Christian faith." A suffering God the Son, rejected by humanity and killed in God the Father's apparent absence (see chapter 5) demands a faith not in accord with human desire. "For the disciples who had followed Jesus to Jerusalem, his shameful death was not the consummation of his obedience to God nor a demonstration of martyrdom for his truth, but the rejection of his claim. It did not confirm their hopes in him, but . . . destroyed them."[45]

As such, the preaching of the cross was a strange foundational element for the Christian church. "The cross," Paul wrote, "is folly to those who are perishing, but to us who are being saved it is the power of God." It was "a stumbling block to Jews and folly to Gentiles" (1 Cor. 1:18, 23).

In Jewish understanding, anyone executed by crucifixion was rejected by his people, cursed by the law of God, and excluded from God's covenant with the Jewish people (Gal. 3:13; Deut. 21:23). They expected, in the light of the main line of Old Testament prophecy, that their Messiah would be a mighty king who would vanquish their enemies. No wonder Christ's cross was "a stumbling block" to them.

The Gentiles saw the cross as the most degrading form of human death. Roman citizens were generally immune from crucifixion. Only the lowest social types received death on a cross. We see the foolishness of the cross to the Gentile world illustrated by a second-century Roman piece of anti-Christian graffiti that depicts a figure with the head of an ass being crucified. A second figure stands alongside with a raised arm. Unevenly scribbled underneath are the words "Alexamenos worships his god."

Perspective

It was the "symbol of defeat," the cross, that became foundational to the message of the first Christian preachers. The cross and the Resurrection, not the perfect life of Christ, formed the heart of the apostolic gospel message (1 Cor. 15:3, 4; Acts 2:23, 24; 3:15).

The apostles did not see the significance of Christ as that of being a superb teacher, but of being a great Savior—a Savior who died for our sins that we might partake of His righteousness. That message changed the world. The centrality of the cross to Christianity led Moltmann to declare that "in Christianity the cross is the test of everything which deserves to be called Christian."[46]

The vicarious sacrifice of Christ, claims Benjamin Warfield, provides the fundamental difference between all types of paganism and Christianity. "Christianity did not come into the world to proclaim a new morality," but to present the Christ who died for our sin. "It is this which differentiates Christianity from all other religions."[47] Thus Ellen White could write that "the sacrifice of Christ as an atonement for sin is the great truth around which all other truths cluster. In order to be rightly understood and appreciated, every truth in the Word of God, from Genesis to Revelation, must be studied in the light that streams from the cross of Calvary. . . . The Son of God uplifted on the cross. This is to be the foundation of every discourse given by our ministers."[48]

And yet the idea of substitutionary sacrifice is what so much modern Christianity seeks to push into the background or to do away with altogether by making Jesus simply an ethical teacher and a perfect example. Yes, Jesus was a great teacher and a sinless example who motivates us to love God and obey His law, but if that is all He was, we are still lost in our sins and under divine condemnation. Removing Christ's substitutionary death from the Bible destroys the central fact of the plan of salvation.

When it comes to Christ's substitutionary sacrifice, human reason and biblical revelation meet head-on. At that very point, Alister McGrath writes, "the cross passes judgment upon the theological competence of human reason by demonstrating that what reason regards as folly hides the wisdom of God."[49]

At Christ's cross the proud heart, which insists on paying for what humans have done, encounters its own bankruptcy.

---

[1] Derek Kidner, *Genesis*, Tyndale Old Testament Commentaries (Downers Grove, Ill.: InterVarsity, 1967), p. 72. Cf. H. C. Leupold, *Exposition of Genesis*, (Grand Rapids: Baker, 1942), vol. 1, p. 179.

[2] White, *Patriarchs and Prophets*, pp. 71, 68.

[3] Vincent Taylor, *Jesus and His Sacrifice* (London: Macmillan, 1943), p. 49. Cf. Gordon J. Wenham, *Numbers*, Tyndale Old Testament Commentaries (Downers Grove, Ill.:

InterVarsity, 1981), p. 202.

[4] Robinson, *Redemption and Revelation*, p. 249.

[5] While the confession of sins in connection with the laying of hands on the sacrificial victim appears only in Lev. 16:21, it seems to be implied in the other passages, and there are references to the combined practice in later times. Leon Morris has noted that "it is not easy to see what the laying on of hands means if there is no symbolic transfer to the animal which was to die of the sins being confessed" (*The Atonement*, pp. 47, 71).

[6] Gordon J. Wenham, *The Book of Leviticus*, New International Commentary on the Old Testament (Grand Rapids: Eerdmans, 1979), pp. 57, 58. For a comprehensive study of the meaning of Old Testament substitution, see Angel M. Rodriguez, *Substitution in the Hebrew Cultus* (Berrien Springs, Mich.: Andrews University Press, 1979).

[7] Stott, *Cross of Christ*, p. 138.

[8] Forsyth, *Cruciality of the Cross*, p. 89.

[9] Wenham suggests that the meaning of the word used for "atonement" in Lev. 17:11 can be translated as "to wipe clean," "to ransom," or "to cover" (*Leviticus*, p. 59). See Edward Heppenstall (*Our High Priest* [Washington, D.C.: Review and Herald, 1972], pp. 25-32) for the wider meaning of the term as reconciliation or at-one-ment.

[10] J. S. Whale, *Victor and Victim: The Christian Doctrine of Redemption* (Cambridge, Eng.: Cambridge University Press, 1960), p. 42.

[11] Moltmann's descriptive phrase from the title of his book.

[12] John Murray, *Redemption Accomplished and Applied* (Grand Rapids: Eerdmans, 1955), p. 27.

[13] McDonald, *Atonement of the Death of Christ*, p. 76.

[14] Hastings Rashdall, *The Idea of Atonement in Christian Theology* (London: Macmillan, 1919), p. 45.

[15] John Macquarrie, *Principles of Christian Theology*, 2nd ed. (New York: Charles Scribner's Sons, 1977), p. 322; cf. p. 314 and Robert S. Franks, *The Atonement* (London: Oxford University Press, 1934), p. 165.

[16] Wilson, *Problem of the Cross*, p. 40.

[17] Horace Bushnell, *The Vicarious Sacrifice* (London: Richard D. Dickinson, 1892), p. 450.

[18] Franks, *The Atonement*, pp. 165-167.

[19] Leslie D. Weatherhead, *A Plain Man Looks at the Cross* (London: Wyvern Books, 1961), p. 71.

[20] James Denney, *The Atonement and the Modern Mind* (New York: A. C. Armstrong and Son, 1903), p. 31.

[21] Brunner, *The Mediator*, pp. 456, 457.

[22] Benjamin Breckinridge Warfield, *The Person and Work of Christ* (Philadelphia: Presbyterian and Reformed, 1970), p. 530. Cf. J. Gresham Machen, *Christianity and Liberalism* (Grand Rapids: Eerdmans, 1946), p. 160.

[23] See chapter 1, notes 8 and 9.

[24] Macquarrie, *Principles of Christian Theology*, p. 315.

[25] William Newton Clarke, *An Outline of Christian Theology* (New York: Charles Scribner's Sons, 1898), p. 331.

[26] Hans K. LaRondelle, *Christ Our Salvation* (Mountain View, Calif.: Pacific Press, 1980), p. 27.

[27] James Stalker, *The Atonement* (New York: American Tract Society, 1909), p. 49.

[28] Machen, *Christianity and Liberalism*, p. 117.

[29] Luther: *Letters of Spiritual Counsel*, ed. Theodore G. Tappert (Philadelphia: Westminster, 1955), p. 110; Luther, in Paul Althaus, *The Theology of Martin Luther*, trans. Robert C. Schultz, (Philadelphia: Fortress, 1966), p. 213; cf. pp. 202-208.

The Cross of Christ

[30] White, *The Desire of Ages*, p. 25.

[31] Ellen G. White, *Steps to Christ* (Mountain View, Calif.: Pacific Press, 1958), pp. 14, 32.

[32] Peter Taylor Forsyth, *The Work of Christ* (London: Hodder and Stoughton, n.d.), p. 83.

[33] Denney, *Christian Doctrine of Reconciliation*, pp. 282, 283; Leon Morris, *The Cross in the New Testament* (Grand Rapids: Eerdmans, 1965), p. 405.

[34] Jack Provonsha, *You Can Go Home Again* (Washington, D.C.: Review and Herald, 1982), p. 36.

[35] Michael Green, *The Empty Cross of Jesus* (Downers Grove, Ill.: InterVarsity, 1984), pp. 78, 79.

[36] Stott, *Cross of Christ*, p. 88.

[37] Paul Tillich, *Systematic Theology* (Chicago: University of Chicago Press, 1951-1963), vol. 2, p. 172.

[38] Morris, *Cross of Jesus*, p. 10.

[39] Stott, *Cross of Christ*, p. 134.

[40] Ellen G. White, MS 50, 1900.

[41] Brunner, *The Mediator*, p. 472.

[42] Forsyth, *Work of Christ*, pp. 182-190.

[43] Friedrich Büchsel, *"Hilastērion,"* in *Theological Dictionary of the New Testament*, ed. G. Kittel and G. Friedrich, vol. 3, p. 322.

[44] On the nature of crucifixion, see Pierson Parker, "Crucifixion," in *The Interpreter's Dictionary of the Bible*, ed. G. A. Buttrick, vol. 1, p. 747; Martin Hengel, *Crucifixion* (Philadelphia: Fortress Press, 1977).

[45] Moltmann, *The Crucified God*, pp. 37, 132.

[46] *Ibid.*, p. 7.

[47] Warfield, *Person and Work of Christ*, p. 425.

[48] Ellen G. White, *Gospel Workers* (Washington, D.C.: Review and Herald, 1948), p. 315.

[49] McGrath, *Mystery of the Cross*, p. 139.

Chapter 4

God in Search of Rebels

In chapter 2 we noted that humanity is in trouble both individually and as a social whole. The results of human rebellion against God have been alienation in all our relationships, a slavery to sin that we are powerless to free ourselves from, a defilement that we cannot cleanse, the penalty of death, and the wrath of God.

In chapter 3 we began to examine God's program for solving the sin problem. At the very base of the plan of salvation in both the Old and New Testaments is the blunt reality of substitutionary sacrifice. Christ did not come primarily as a great teacher or as an example of what our lives can be like, but as a Savior who died on the cross in our place. The sacrificial death of Christ is not simply a constituent part of Christianity. To the contrary, Christ's substitutionary sacrifice is its very essence. Without His vicarious sacrifice there would be no Christianity.

The present chapter will explore further God's plan for saving us from the results of sin by looking into some of the powerful picture-words that the Bible writers used to describe Christ's work for lost sinners. Understanding such words as "propitiation," "redemption," "justification," "reconciliation," "cleansing," and their cognates is important as we seek to come to grips with what God is trying to do for us through Christ.

Such images help us understand the process of salvation, but we should remember that they are metaphors rather than exact descriptions of what took place. They are each capable of explaining some facet of truth, but no one metaphor is "the full answer" to what Christ did for us, nor do even all of them combined provide us with a complete understanding. Each expresses a truth about Christ's work, all complement the others, but the truth of what Christ accomplished is far more comprehensive than either their individual and composite suggestions. Viewed within their purposes and limitations, however, such biblical word pictures of Christ's work for us shed much light on the plan of salvation.

The Cross of Christ

We should note that "sacrifice" is not one of these word pictures. We saw in chapter 3 that the language of substitutionary sacrifice permeates the symbolism of both Testaments. John Stott is correct when he contends that "'substitution' is not a further 'theory' or 'image' to be set alongside the others, but rather the foundation of them all."[1]

A further point to keep in mind before we examine the graphic word pictures of salvation is that they have a common denominator in God's love. The basic fact undergirding each of them is that "God so loved the world that he gave his only Son, that whoever believes in him should not perish but have eternal life. For God sent the Son into the world, not to condemn the world, but that the world might be saved through him" (John 3:16, 17).

God's purpose is not to see how many individuals He can consign to hell. Rather, in His aggressive, saving love He is out to seek and to save as many as possible (Luke 19:10). The comforting truth is that He does not function in the plan of salvation as a passive spectator, but as the God of caring action. One of the supreme truths of Scripture is that it was the Father who provided the Savior. Octavius Winslow put it succinctly when he wrote: "Who delivered up Jesus to die? Not Judas, for money; not Pilate, for fear; not the Jews, for envy—but the Father, for love!"[2]

Three of the salvational word pictures we will discuss appear in the tightly-packed verses of Romans 3:23-26. Paul writes that those who believe in Christ "are *justified* by his grace as a gift, through the *redemption* which is in Christ Jesus, whom God put forward as an *expiation [propitiation]* by his blood, to be received by faith. This was *to show [demonstrate] God's righteousness [justice],* because in his divine forbearance he had passed over former sins; it was *to prove* at the present time *that he himself is righteous [just] and that he justifies him who has faith in Jesus.*" Our fourth word picture, *reconciliation,* Paul emphasizes in such texts as Romans 5:10; 2 Corinthians 5:19, 20; and Colossians 1:20, while a fifth, *cleansing* or *purification,* is at the center of the book of Hebrews.

Propitiation

Of all the words used in Romans 3:23-26, the Greek word translated in the King James Version as "propitiation" has been the most unpopular. It creates such a negative reaction, in fact, that nearly all modern translations avoid it entirely.

One reason that makes propitiation an unpopular word is its connection with the idea of the wrath of God. As we noted in chapter 2, many modern religious scholars and laypeople would rather see the wrath of God as the impersonal outworking of the results of sin than as the righteous "vengeance" of a holy God. Those who take the impersonal view of wrath have no need for the concept of propitiation.

Even more damning for the use of propitiation is its basic meaning of "turning away wrath." In the Greek world in which the New Testament arose, propitiation had the flavor of bribing the gods, demons, or the dead in an attempt to win their favor and get their blessing. Since the gods were "mad," they had to be appeased. Thus people offered sacrifices in an attempt to please the supernatural beings, buy back their favor, and avert their wrath.[3]

We find that type of propitiation in the Old Testament when the king of Moab, seeing the battle was going against him, offered "his eldest son who was to reign in his stead" as a "burnt offering" to Chemosh in the hope of winning his favor (2 Kings 3:26, 27). The Israelites, imbibing some of the religious ideas of their neighbors, were tempted to perform the same type of propitiatory acts (see 2 Kings 16:3; 21:2, 6; Jer. 7:31; 19:4-6; Micah 6:7). On a human level, the equivalent for propitiation appears in Genesis 32:20, in which Jacob sought to "appease" or "pacify" Esau with a present.

It is not surprising that such crude pictures have led Bible translators away from using propitiation, with its allusions to bribery and averting wrath. They have opted for softer words.

The problem with the softer words, however, is that they do not reflect biblical reality. As we noted in chapter 2, *God is angry and His anger is personal and active.* He is deadly serious about sin. It hurts His caring heart to see the people whom He so lovingly created be destroyed. His wrath against sin is the natural result. Scripture describes even the loving Jesus as a wrathful Lamb who will eventually be "revealed from heaven with his mighty angels in flaming fire, inflicting vengeance upon those who do not know God and upon those who do not obey the gospel of our Lord Jesus. They shall suffer the punishment of eternal destruction and exclusion from the presence of the Lord and from the glory of his might" (2 Thess. 1:7-9; see also Rev. 6:16).

Wrath and love are not opposites. To the contrary, God's wrath, as we saw in chapter 2, is a product of His love. *His wrath is His judgment on sin.* Repeatedly the Old Testament declares that God is slow to anger (Ex. 34:6; Neh. 9:17; and others), but even though it is slow, His anger is real. The New Testament teaches that divine wrath is certain for those who continue in sin.

The Cross of Christ

Leon Morris writes that *if God's "wrath is regarded as a very real factor so that the sinner is exposed to its severity, then the removal of the wrath will be an important part of our understanding of salvation."* Of course, "if we diminish the part played by divine wrath we shall not find it necessary to think seriously of propitiation."[4] Thus Morris comments in another connection, "if people are to be forgiven, then the fact of that wrath must be taken into consideration. It does not fade away by being given some other name or regarded as an impersonal process."[5] In other words, God's wrath must be propitiated or turned away from the sinner. That was one aim of Christ's self-sacrifice on the cross.

That thought brings us back to Romans 3:25. For the first two and a half chapters of Romans Paul has been building up his case that because of universal human guilt ("all have sinned" [Rom. 3:23]), all humanity—both Jew and Gentile—is under divine condemnation and wrath. The problems that God faces are how He can save sinners and still remain just, and on what basis He can save them.

Part of the complex answer is propitiation. Perhaps at this juncture a reading of the New International Version's translation of Romans 3:25 will help us understand biblical propitiation better. "God presented him [Jesus] *as a sacrifice of atonement* [propitiation], through faith in his blood." The NIV marginal reading is even more helpful: "God presented him *as the one who would turn aside his wrath, taking away sin* through faith in his blood." Thus the NIV equates propitiation with a "sacrifice of atonement," or the turning aside of God's wrath. In other words, Christ bore the wrath of God on Calvary. His death propitiated or turned away the wrath of God from those who believe in Him by faith.

"It is impossible," wrote William Sanday and A. C. Headlam in their highly regarded commentary on Romans, "to get rid from this passage of the double idea (1) of a sacrifice; (2) of a sacrifice which is propitiatory,"[6]

John 3:36 needs to be understood in the light of the above facts: "He who believes in the Son has eternal life; he who does not obey the Son shall not see life, but the wrath of God rests upon him." That statement is true because Jesus bore God's judgment on sin (wrath) and the penalty for sin on the cross[7] for (in the place of) those who believe in Him. He tasted the cup of wrath for all humanity. And for those who by faith accept His sacrifice, He has absorbed the just penalty for the rebellious disregard of God's person and law, which had threatened the moral stability of the universe.

As James Denney puts it, His was "a death in which the divine condemnation of sin comes upon Christ, and is exhausted there, so that there is thenceforth no more condemnation for those that are in Him" (cf. Rom. 8:1). "Although Christ was not punished by God," P. T. Forsyth asserts, "He bore God's penalty upon sin."[8]

When using such concepts as "wrath," "propitiation," "penalty," "death," "blood," and "sacrifice," the Bible comes to grips with the hard facts of sin and its consequences for both diety and humanity. In God's eyes sin is not a trifling matter that He can lightly dismiss, letting bygones be bygones. Sin destroys lives, and its insidious nature threatens cosmic trust in God. God chose not to sit idly by while sin destroyed His creation. He has condemned sin to death wherever found. Human beings have, as we have seen, come under that sentence.

The work of salvation must deal with this justly deserved condemnation of sin and sinners. Some have held, as we noted in chapter 3, that what Christ's work needed to accomplish was to overcome our distrust of God. Thus they picture His role as primarily demonstrating God's character so that people can trust Him. That theory, while having some merit, flies in the face of the Bible's *brutal* portrayal of the problem and of the divine solution.

While Christ's death reveals God's love to us, it does much more than that—it removes the sentence of God's just condemnation from us. James Denney nicely illustrates the shallowness of the teaching that claims that a propitiation (turning away) of God's wrath (judgment) was unnecessary—that Jesus died primarily to demonstrate God's love for humanity. "If," Denney writes, "I were sitting on the end of the pier, on a summer day, enjoying the sunshine and the air, and some one [sic] came along and jumped into the water and got drowned 'to prove his love for me,' I should find it quite unintelligible. I might be much in need of love, but an act in no rational relation to any of my necessities could not prove it. But if I had fallen over the pier and were drowning, and some one [sic] sprang into the water, and at the cost of making my peril, or what but for him would be my fate, his own, saved me from death, then I should say, 'Greater love hath no man than this [John 15:13].' I should say it intelligibly, because there would be an intelligible relation between the sacrifice which love made and the necessity from which it redeemed."[9]

The thing that God had to accomplish through the work of Christ, Denney suggests, was not overcoming "man's distrust of God, but God's condemnation of man. . . . He puts it [our condemnation] away by bearing it. He removes it from us by taking it upon Himself." The really important thing in the New Testament is that Christ's work fully and finally settled the issue between a holy God and human sin. "There could have been," Ellen White wrote, "no pardon for sin had this atonement [of Christ's taking our death 'penalty' for sin on Himself] not been made."[10]

God, as Cosmic Ruler, was not in a position to dismiss His judgment on sin. He had to deal with it responsibly. Thus "Paul speaks of the moral necessity for the sacrifice of the Son of God" in Romans 3:25, 26 "as based not only on God's love but on His righteousness."[11]

The apostle sets forth the "propitiatory sacrifice" of Romans 3:25 as the demonstrated "proof" of God's "righteousness" or "justice." Christ's "sacrifice of atonement" (NIV), which shows God's justice, is crucial to the plan of salvation, because, writes Denney, "there can be no gospel unless there is such a thing as a righteousness of God." God must be proved just if He is to be the justifier of those who have faith in Christ (verse 26). The divine problem in dealing with a sinful race was how to maintain His own justice while clearing the guilty.[12]

God in His mercy, C. E. B. Cranfield concluded from his impressive study of Romans 3:21-26 ("the centre and heart" of Romans), willed not only to forgive sinful human beings, but "to forgive them righteously." He accomplished His goal, without "condoning . . . sin," by directing "against His own very Self in the person of His Son the full weight of that righteous wrath" that sinners deserved. Cranfield therefore viewed Christ as "a propitiatory sacrifice."[13]

Before moving away from the rather difficult concept of propitiation, it is important to recognize that the Bible is clear that Christ's blood was not shed to appease God's wrath. To the contrary, God "put forward" the propitiatory sacrifice (Rom. 3:25). "In this is love," John wrote, "not that we loved God but that he loved us and sent his Son to be the expiation [propitiation] for our sins" (1 John 4:10; cf. John 3:16). The cross, therefore, does not represent a change in God's attitude toward sinners. To the contrary, it is the supreme expression of that love. We read in *Steps to Christ* that *"the Father loves us, not because of the great propitiation, but He provided the propitiation because He loves us."* Thus, Forsyth claims, "the atonement did not procure grace, it flowed from grace."[14]

In the plan of salvation, the loving Son is not pitted against the angry Father on behalf of helpless sinners. Both suffered when Christ bore our condemnation on the cross. "Together," penned Edward Heppenstall, "They bore Their own judgment on sin."[15]

In summary, the Bible is not a pleasant book. It deals with the grim

God in Search of Rebels

realities of life. One of them is God's wrath (His judgment on sin). All humans are under that wrath. God in His love, therefore, sent Christ as a sacrifice to propitiate (turn away) the just requirements of His own wrath. Because Christ bore the penalty for all humans (Heb. 9:12, 26; 10:10, 12-14), those who have faith in Him are safe, but those who reject His grace remain under God's wrath (John 3:36) and will be left to face that wrath at the end of time (Rev. 6:15-17).

Christ's death put God's forgiveness on a moral foundation. Because of the propitiatory sacrifice that demonstrated His consistency and justice, God is free to forgive and justify sinners who accept Christ and still be just Himself. God's love is a moral love. G. C. Berkouwer points out that "divine forgiveness is never, in Scripture, an indifferent love or a matter of God's *being blind*. It is rather a turning from real *wrath* to real *grace*." "What the atonement effects," writes Heppenstall, "is not a change in God but a change in the exercise of judgment upon the sinner, and therefore a change in the relation between God and repentant sinners."[16]

Our brief examination of propitiation has not made the easiest reading, but I trust that it has been helpful. Such discussions, of course, are merely the beginning of our understanding of the topic. "Not in this life," Ellen White writes, "shall we comprehend the mystery of God's love in giving His Son to be the propitiation for our sins. The work of our Redeemer on this earth is and ever will be a subject that will put to the stretch our highest imagination."[17]

Our next word picture, fortunately, is not as foreign to our modern thought patterns as propitiation.

Redemption

If propitiation has to do with the language of the sacrificial altar, redemption leads our minds to the marketplace. While some of us have a great deal of trouble coming to terms with the ideas related to propitiation, we find redemption comparatively easy to understand. In fact, it belongs to a word group that we often use in our daily lives. My mother, for example, used to be a great saver of S&H Green Stamps. For every dime she spent at participating stores she received a stamp, which she pasted into specially made booklets. She also had a catalogue that told her what gifts she could get for a certain number of Green Stamp books. When she finally had enough books filled, she hauled them down to the Green Stamp store, where she could turn them in and "redeem" her gift. The Green Stamp store, interestingly enough, was called a "redemption center."

The Cross of Christ

The most basic meaning of "redeem" is "to buy" or "to buy back." The Bible associates redemption with such related concepts as ransom, purchase, and price.

For us moderns, redemption is largely a theological word, even though we do use it for certain things in our daily lives. But for first-century Jews and Christians, it had a much more active role in daily life.

The use of "redemption" in the universal Greek culture of antiquity had its origin in the practice of warfare. After a battle the victors would round up the vanquished and take them home to sell them as slaves. Sometimes, however, they discovered that they had captured important people who were worth more to their native country than they were as slaves. The victors would let their enemies know of such valuable captives and offered to release them for a price. As a result, many times family members or others would raise money to "buy back" (redeem) those special prisoners of war. The purchase price was called the "ransom."[18]

The ancient Jews were also familiar with the process of redemption. For example, a Hebrew landowner forced to sell his land for financial reasons might "redeem" it at any time (Lev. 25:25; compare Ruth 4:1-10, where Boaz acts as the redeemer for Ruth's property). In a similar manner, if a Jew became poor, he could sell himself into slavery to help clear his indebtedness. Such slavery, however, was not to be permanent. Jewish slaves could be redeemed by a near kinsman ("redeemer" in Hebrew), or if the slave grew rich "he may redeem himself" (Lev. 25:47-49).

God even pictured Himself as a kinsman-redeemer in the Old Testament. "I am the Lord," He told the Hebrew nation enslaved in Egypt, "and I will bring you out from under the burdens of the Egyptians, and I will deliver you from their bondage, and I will redeem you with an outstretched arm and with great acts of judgment" (Ex. 6:6).

The New Testament applies the familiar redemption concept to Christ. As we saw in chapter 2, one of the results of the rebellion against God's rulership was hopeless enslavement to sin and Satan (John 8:34; Titus 3:3; Rom. 6:16). Unlike the Jew who could become rich and redeem himself (Lev. 25:49), however, Satan's captives struggle in vain against the bondage of sin. The spirit of evil does not merely control individuals from the outside (1 John 5:19), but it exists within them as "the lust of the flesh and the lust of the eyes and the pride of life" (1 John 2:16).

Christ took it upon Himself to pay the redemption price for human freedom. "For the Son of man," Jesus told His bickering disciples, "also came not to be served but to serve, and to give his life as a *ransom* for many"

(Mark 10:45). Paul taught the same truth when he wrote of "Christ Jesus, who gave himself as a *ransom* for all" (1 Tim. 2:5, 6). Again Paul wrote: "Christ *redeemed* us from the curse of the law, having become a curse for us" (Gal. 3:13). In like manner, Peter penned that "you were *ransomed* from the futile ways inherited from your fathers, not with perishable things such as silver or gold, but with the precious blood of Christ, like that of a lamb without blemish or spot" (1 Peter 1:18, 19; compare Rev. 5:9).

Ellen White, like Paul in Romans 3:24-26, ties the concept of redemption to Christ's propitiatory sacrifice and the justice of God. "What right," she queried, "had Christ to take the captives out of the enemy's hands? The right of having made a sacrifice that satisfies the principles of justice by which the kingdom of heaven is governed. . . . On the cross of Calvary He paid the redemption price of the race. And thus He gained the right to take the captives from the grasp of the great deceiver, who, by a lie, framed against the government of God, caused the fall of man, and thus forfeited all claim to be called a loyal subject of God's glorious everlasting kingdom. Our ransom has been paid by our Saviour. No one need be enslaved by Satan. Christ stands before us as our all-powerful helper."[19]

According to the New Testament, however, our redemption from sin brings us to the service of a new Master rather than to existential or absolute freedom. "You are not your own," Paul wrote to the Corinthians. "You were bought with a price." Therefore "glorify God in your body" and "shun immorality" (1 Cor. 6:18-20). Christ's redemption is for service to God. As such, it affects every aspect of the Christian life.

We need to emphasize two points regarding Christ's redemption. One is that He willingly "gave" Himself for the task as an act of grace (Mark 10:45; 1 Tim. 2:6). The second is that the ransom price was His "blood" (1 Peter 1:19).

That second point has raised innumerable questions about, and distortions of, the redemption/ransom word picture. Many have asked regarding to whom He paid the ransom. Did Christ have to "pay off" God in bribery fashion?

Most theologians have ruled out payment to God. That, of course, left the devil as the most popular candidate for receiving the purchase price, a solution especially popular from the second through the twelfth centuries. It was generally held that through sin humans had put themselves into the devil's power. Thus the devil, as their lawful possessor, had a just claim for compensation, which God met with Christ's ransom on the cross.

Most agreed, however, that the devil got a bad bargain, since the con-

The Cross of Christ

cealed divinity of Christ in human flesh prevented the devil from holding Him captive. Gregory of Nyssa (c. 330-c. 395), for example, suggested that the devil accepted the offered ransom payment much like a fish takes a baited hook. Since Christ had clothed His divinity with humanity, the devil thought he saw a desirable morsel—one he would have avoided under normal circumstances. Thus as a fish swallows the bait and gets the hook also, so the devil grabbed his prey, and found himself thereby captured by the Godhead. In a similar manner, Augustine (354-430) used the illustration of a mousetrap. As the bait entices mice into the trap, Christ was the bait by which God caught the devil.[20]

Such nonbiblical illustrations overlook the fact that word pictures such as ransom and redemption are metaphors that teach a lesson but (like Christ's parables) were not meant to be taken literally in all their details. We do not, therefore, have to be concerned with whom the ransom payment went to.

Leon Morris writes "that in the New Testament there is never any hint of a recipient of the ransom. In other words[,] we must understand redemption as a useful metaphor which enables us to see some aspects of Christ's great saving work with clarity but which is not an exact description of the whole process of salvation. We must not press it beyond what the New Testament tells us about it. To look for a recipient of the ransom is illegitimate. We have no reason for pressing every detail. We must use the metaphor in the way the New Testament writers did or we fall into error."[21]

As a word picture, redemption helps us understand the work of Christ on the cross in at least two ways. First, it graphically portrays one result of salvation—it has freed sinners from slavery to sin. Second, it brings us face to face with the almost unbelievable cost of that freedom—a price no less than that of the blood of Christ on Calvary (1 Peter 1:18, 19; Gal. 1:4; 2:20; Eph. 5:2, 25; Titus 2:14). As Norman Gulley put it, grace was not cheap. "Calvary constitutes the most expensive price ever paid for anything."[22]

Before moving away from the redemption metaphor, we should note that whereas the redemption price was paid in full at the time of the cross, the Bible also speaks of redemption as being future (Eph. 4:30; Rom. 8:23). The point is that in the present life we see no more than the beginning of what redemption means. Only after Christ comes again shall we know its meaning in all its fullness.

Justification

The third expressive metaphor of salvation found in Romans 3:24-26 is justification. God's solutions are designed to meet the human crises (discussed in chapter 2) that resulted from sin. We have seen that propitiation refers to the averting of God's wrath and that redemption reflects freedom from bondage to sin. By contrast, Paul coined the metaphor of justification to meet the problem of the legal curse of the law with its death penalty.

While propitiation took us to the world of the sacrificial altar and redemption to that of the marketplace, justification brings us to the courtroom. The problem that justification faces is that all people have sinned (Rom. 3:23) and are therefore under condemnation, even to the point of death (Rom. 6:23). "Justification," Vincent Taylor claimed, "is a question first and last of man's *standing* with God." Is a person righteous or guilty before the divine Judge?[23]

In Romans 3 justification does not mean "to make righteous," but rather "to declare righteous." "The root idea in justification," George Eldon Ladd writes, "is the declaration of God, the righteous judge, that the man who believes in Christ, sinful though he may be, . . . is viewed as being righteous, because in Christ he has come into a righteous relationship with God." Even beyond that, God treats justified individuals as if they were righteous. Relationship, Ladd suggests, is the key to understanding justification. "The justified man has, in Christ, entered into a new relationship with God," who now regards such a person as righteous and treats that individual accordingly. The new relationship that brings justification, we should note, does not make a person intrinsically righteous, but it is *"real righteousness"* because a person's relationship to God in Christ is real. *Justification is the opposite of condemnation*. "It is the decree of acquittal from all guilt and issues in freedom from all condemnation and punishment."[24]

The ground of justification is, as Paul points out, Christ's death (Rom. 5:9; 3:24, 25). The means by which it becomes effective for the individual is faith (Rom. 5:1; 3:25; Gal. 2:16, 20; Phil. 3:9). Although people do have a legal relationship to God, it is also true that that relationship is much more than just a legal one. God's love for humanity impels Him to give people what they do not deserve (grace). Thus God's plan of salvation rests upon His grace (Rom. 3:24; Eph. 2:8). As a result, Paul says that God "justifies the ungodly" (Rom. 4:5; 5:6, 8, 10).

Interestingly enough, His legal practices are just the opposite of the instructions He gave for human judges, who were to "justify the righteous, and condemn the wicked" (Deut. 25:1, KJV). Anyone who "justifies the wicked," we read in Proverbs, and "condemns the righteous" is "an abomination to the Lord" (Prov. 17:15).

The issue that we must face at this point is how God can break the rules that He set forth for human judges. It is that type of problem, Morris claims, that troubles Paul in Romans 3. How can God be righteous if He forgives people who have no right to be forgiven? One would expect a just God to punish those who deserved it. That is what justice means. But in the past, Paul claims in verse 25, God did not invariably punish sin. Sinners went on living.

"Now," Morris suggests, "you can argue that this shows God to be merciful, or compassionate, or kind, or forbearing, or loving. But you cannot argue that it shows him to be *just*." Because God had not always punished sinners, some would be tempted to doubt His justice. "Not anymore," Paul declares in Romans 3:24-26. "The cross demonstrates the righteousness, the justice of God. . . . It is not the fact that God forgives that shows him to be righteous, but the fact that he forgives in a certain way, the way of the cross. . . . God does not set aside the moral law when he forgives." To the contrary, Paul contends that God forgives in all justice because of Christ's death on the cross that took the moral structure of the universe into consideration.[25]

At the cross the entire universe saw the outworking of the kingdoms of good and evil. There God demonstrated that He could be trusted, and Satan proved that he indeed was a liar and a murderer (John 8:44) when he took the life of the sinless Son of God, the one person in history who was beyond sin's death penalty (chapter 5 will expand this point). It was in the brutal fact of the cross that God showed that He was both just and loving, and that His creation could have confidence in His way since He was willing to sacrifice of Himself for the good of the universe. The Godhead laid the ground for forgiveness and justification at the cross. Because of the cross, God could justify and still be just Himself. At the cross He demonstrated His goodness and mercy, which "could be called in question by His passing over sins committed" up to that time (Rom. 3:25, 26).[26] Thus at the cross God provided the basis for not only justifying sinners up through that historic point, but also in the future if they were willing to accept Christ's work for them by faith.

D. Martyn Lloyd-Jones sets forth the importance of Romans 3:26 when he points out that verses 25 and 26 highlight something "infinitely more important" than the justification of human beings. "The Cross is the vindication of the character of God. The Cross not only shows the love of God more gloriously than anything else, it shows His righteousness, His justice, His holiness. . . . On Calvary God was making a way of salvation so that you and I might be forgiven. But He had to do so in a way that will leave His character inviolate. . . . God was declaring publicly once and for ever His eternal justice AND His eternal love. Never separate them, for they belong together."[27]

A similar teaching on the justice or righteousness of God in forgiving sinners occurs in 1 John 1:9, which reads: "If we confess our sins, he is faithful and *just*, and will forgive our sins and cleanse us from all unrighteousness." On this verse John Stott observes that "it is not difficult to see why God is said to be 'faithful' in forgiving our sins. But how can he also be described as *just* when he forgives us our sins?" To Stott "just" is a "strange adjective" that points to the "divine dilemma" of God giving sinners what they don't deserve. "The cross," he concludes, "is, in fact, the only moral ground on which he can forgive sin at all. . . . He is *faithful* to forgive because he has promised to do so, and *just* because his Son died for our sins."[28]

Colin Kruse uplifts the same theme in comparing the teaching of Romans 3:25, 26 on the justification or righteousness of God with that of 1 John 1:9, noting that "the author of 1 John does not state the matter as clearly as Paul does, but it is plain that he, too, understands God to be righteous in forgiving those who confess their sins because he sent his Son to be the atoning sacrifice (*hilasmos*) for those sins (cf. 2:2)."[29]

Justification, like the other symbols of salvation, flows from God's grace. As God searched for Adam in Eden, so He took the initiative in sending Christ to die for us while we were still His enemies (Rom. 5:6, 10). As with the other metaphors, the concept of justification does raise problems, but it also contributes insights into the plan of salvation that no other word picture provides.

Reconciliation

Sin, Brunner suggests, "is like the son who strikes his father's face in anger; . . . it is the bold self-assertion of the son's will above that of the father."[30] The need for reconciliation is rooted in the broken relationship between God and humanity, which has resulted in alienation between persons and God, people from each other, individuals from their own selves, and the race from the world of nature (see chapter 2).

"'Reconciliation,'" Karl Barth noted, "is the restitution, the resumption of a fellowship which once existed but was then threatened by dissolution." The Bible always views reconciliation in terms of God's covenant relationship to us, a broken relationship that needs restoration.[31] Reconciliation has the same meaning today as it did in Bible times—to restore a relationship, to renew a friendship.

With reconciliation we leave behind the language of the altar, the marketplace, and the law court, and turn to the family circle—a circle shattered by the rebellion of sin. The term "reconciliation" is about as close as we can come to understanding one of the great central meanings of atonement—that of "at-one-ment." The significance of the concept is that of being at-one again with God, our fellows, our selves, and God's creation.[32] While only Paul uses the words translated as reconciliation, and then not very often, the concept they represent underlies the entire Bible from Genesis through Revelation, from Eden lost to Eden restored.

Paul always speaks of people being reconciled to God (2 Cor. 5:19; Rom. 5:10; Col. 1:20). He never refers to God being reconciled to us. In spite of that fact, however, we should recognize that sin affected both sides.[33] Humanity's rebellion and sense of guilt alienated it from God, while God was separated from humankind by His necessary hatred of and judgment on sin (His wrath). Christ's sacrificial death (propitiation) removed the barrier to reconciliation from God's side.[34] It is significant that the connection between propitiation and reconciliation appears in each of Paul's important statements on the topic. In Romans 5:10 he says that "we were reconciled to God by the death of his Son." Ephesians 2:16 ties reconciliation to the cross, Colossians 1:20 to "the blood of his cross," and 2 Corinthians 5:19, 21 to Christ's sin bearing.

Thus Christ's "sacrifice of atonement" (Rom. 3:25, NIV) laid the foundation for God to reach out to us in graceful reconciliation. The change in God, Vincent Taylor wrote, "is not a change from hostility to love, but from the love which judges and condemns to a love which welcomes and receives men into fellowship with Himself."[35]

Because Christ's sacrificial propitiation and the related reality of justification are foundational to God's reaching out to humanity, reconciliation is primarily a movement of God toward humanity. That does not mean that people have no part. Each person's role is one of response to God's gracious offer. Those who do so positively are adopted back into God's household (Gal. 4:5; Eph. 1:5; John 1:12), but "if a man refuses to enter into the reconciliation with God," W. L. Walker writes, "he remains where he stood, under the operation of that 'wrath' or judgment-element which belongs essentially to the Righteousness and Love of God."[36]

The positive results of reconciliation are many. One is "peace with God" (Col. 1:20; Rom. 5:1), stemming from the fact that the reconciled no longer have God "counting their trespasses against them," because He made Christ "to be sin who knew no sin, so that in him we might become the righteousness of God" (2 Cor. 5:18-21).

A second blessing is "access" to God's grace and blessings (Rom. 5:2). This access to God is closely related to the reconciled person being adopted back into His covenant family (Gal. 4:5; John 1:12). Thus we, having been "born anew" (John 3:3, 5), can call God our Father (Matt. 6:9). Since "reconciliation is a state, and not only an act,"[37] Paul can speak repeatedly of the saved being "in Christ" (Rom. 6:11; 8:1; 1 Cor. 1:30; 1 Thess. 1:1), and John can talk of "abiding in him" (John 6:56; 15:5-7; 1 John 2:6, 24, 27, 28).

Because of their reconciled status, God's restored children can live in a state of "fellowship" and "communion" with Him (1 Cor. 1:9; 10:16; Phil. 3:10; 1 John 1:3, 6). Restored access to God and adoption into His family means, as it did for the prodigal son, full access to and possession of God's covenant blessings (Luke 15:20-23).

A third result of reconciliation is joy (Rom. 5:2, 11).

A fourth is that it reconciles us not only to God but to our fellow human beings by breaking down the "dividing wall of hostility" that alienates races, peoples, and individuals from each other (Eph. 2:14-16). It is impossible to be reconciled to God without being re-united with our neighbors.

More comprehensive is the fact that the reconciled are "new creations" (2 Cor. 5:17). Being brought back into harmony with God, therefore, affects every part of their lives from their motivations to their actions in every sphere of existence.

Most important is that the reconciliation made available by Christ's sacrifice leads to cosmic peace as it clears God's universe of rebellion and its results. Thus Paul could write: "Through him God chose to reconcile the whole universe to himself, making peace through the shedding of his blood upon the cross—to reconcile all things, whether on earth or in heaven, through him alone" (Col. 1:20, NEB).

Reconciliation is a present Christian reality, but its fullness and completeness will happen only after the destruction of sin and the establishment of God's New Jerusalem (Rev. 20-22). The Bible's last two chapters represent the complete healing of all humanity's alienations that entered in through the rebellion of Genesis 3.

Cleansing

Cleansing from defilement is the metaphor for salvation most neglected by modern writers on the atonement. But the author of the book of Hebrews certainly didn't ignore it. To the contrary, he puts it up front and makes it a central theme in his presentation. When Christ "had made *purification* for sins," we read in the epistle's preface, "he sat down at the right hand of the Majesty on high" (Heb. 1:3). That is not an isolated idea. We find the apostle returning to the topic of cleansing from sin and its results in such passages as Hebrews 9:13, 14, 22, 23; 10:2, 22. And it is no accident that most of his references to cleansing show up in chapters 9 and 10. Up to that point Hebrews had set forth two covenants, two sanctuaries, and two priesthoods. In each case the one connected to Christ was better than the one provided through the Levitical system. But with Hebrews 9:11-14 the Epistle begins to present two sacrifices, one that really can't solve the core of the defilement by sin problem and one that can (see verses 13, 14).

William Johnsson notes that "if Christ is to solve the cosmic predicament, He must be able to purify"[38] from the deadly defilement of sin. And, as with the other metaphors of atonement set forth in the New Testament, the means of Christ's cleansing from sin is His blood shed "once for all" on Calvary. As Hebrews 9:12 puts it, "He entered once for all into the Holy Place [of the heavenly sanctuary], taking not the blood of goats and calves but his own blood, thus securing an eternal redemption" (cf. Heb. 7:27; 9:26-28; 10:10).

Repeatedly the book of Hebrews sets forth blood as the means of purification.

• "For if the sprinkling of defiled persons with the blood of goats and bulls and with the ashes of a heifer sanctifies for the purification of the flesh, how much more shall the *blood of Christ*, who through the eternal Spirit offered himself without blemish to God, *purify* your conscience from dead works to serve the living God" (Heb. 9:13, 14).

• "Under the law almost everything is *purified with blood*" (verse 22).

• "Thus it was necessary for the copies of the heavenly things to be *purified* with these rites, but the heavenly things themselves with *better sacrifices* than these" (verse 23).

• Concerning the ineffectiveness of the Levitical sacrifices, Hebrews 10:2 notes that "if the worshipers had once been *cleansed*, they would no longer have any consciousness of sin."

• But the sacrifice and ministry of Christ is truly effective. As a result, verse 22 tells Christians that they can "draw near [to God] with a true heart in full assurance of faith, with our hearts sprinkled [an allusion to the sprinkling of blood in the Old Testament sanctuary service] *clean* from an evil conscience."

These and other passages leave us without the slightest doubt that the book of Hebrews has a deep concern with defilement and cleansing. The Old Testament repeatedly tied the "defilement/blood/purification" theme to the sanctuary. The book of Hebrews, being the fullest treatment of the heavenly sanctuary, unites those concerns in the New Testament. It is no accident, given its focus, that Hebrews "identifies Christ's achievement as *making purification* for sins" in its introductory verses (see 1:3).[39] Other places in the New Testament, such as 1 John 1:9 and Titus 2:14, utilize the cleansing metaphor, but Hebrews is the one New Testament book that puts it at the center.

In summing up the contribution of the book of Hebrews on the topic, Johnsson writes that "sin is a moral problem, not to be removed by mechanical shedding of animal blood. It is a hideous defilement, separating us from God's holiness. Only God can supply the answer and bring radical purification. And this He did in the gift of Jesus Christ, He who is both Sacrifice and High Priest."[40]

The book of Hebrews makes it clear beyond the shadow of a doubt that cleansing is an accomplished fact consummated on the cross. "When he *had made purification* for sins, he sat down at the right hand of the Majesty on high" (Heb. 1:3).

But like the other metaphors of atonement, that accomplishment did not mean that belief in Christ fully removed sin from believers' lives. Just as Paul can say that "Christ redeemed us from the curse of the law" by His sacrifice on the cross (Gal. 3:13) yet also speak of full redemption as yet future (Eph. 4:30; Rom. 8:23), so can Hebrews set forth cleansing as both an accomplished fact and an ongoing process. After all, Christ "always lives to make intercession" (Heb. 7:25) and He is "a minister in the sanctuary and the true tent" (Heb. 8:2). In His great once for all sacrifice "He provided the great means for [defilement's] removal,"[41] but the universe will not be entirely clean until the final destruction of sin. Thus we and Scripture can speak of the cleansing work of Christ as both completed but not yet finished.

One passage that has caused a great deal of discussion and consternation among Christian commentators is Hebrews 9:23, which plainly states that heavenly things need to be purified with better sacrifices than those of sheep and goats. William Lane of Seattle Pacific University points out that although some have dismissed the implications of that text as "'nonsense,'" the verse "clearly implies that the heavenly sanctuary had also become defiled by the sin of the people." Lane goes on to note that that wider defilement removes the issues of the cleansing metaphor from the merely individual or even earthly realm and places it in a galactic context.[42]

Lutheran scholar Craig Koester moves beyond Lane when he observes that "if the earthly sanctuary is a representation of the heavenly one (8:2, 5), then laws pertaining to the earthly tent presumably disclose something about the heavenly tent that it represents. One might conclude that the earthly sanctuary was cleansed because its heavenly counterpart also was to be cleansed. Christ did not purify the heavenly sanctuary because he was bound to follow the Levitical pattern; rather, the reverse is true. Levitical practice foreshadows Christ's cleansing of the heavenly tent."[43]

It is beyond the scope of the book of Hebrews to establish the time of the cleansing of the heavenly. Koester places it at the cross, but if one follows his typological logic it would not be completed until the Second Advent, at which time the problem of ongoing sinful defilement comes to an end for all eternity.

Perspective

We have explored five of the central New Testament word pictures of salvation. The Bible writers took them from the shrine, the marketplace, the law court, and the family. John Stott outlines[44] several themes that emerge from four of those symbolic word pictures. (We should observe that while he does not mention cleansing, everything he says about the other four could also apply to the cleansing symbol.)

First, each meets a different aspect of human need. *Propitiation* rescues us from the wrath of God, *redemption* from our captivity to sin, *justification* from our guilt and condemnation, and *reconciliation* from our enmity against God and our manifold alienations.

Second, the metaphors emphasize God's saving initiative of grace, growing out of His love. "It is he," writes Stott, "who has propitiated his own wrath, redeemed us from our miserable bondage, declared us righteous in his sight, and reconciled us to himself." As Richard Rice put it, "Atonement is not something an angry God demands, but something a loving God provides."[45]

Third, all four images teach that God achieved His saving work through the blood of Christ in His substitutionary sacrifice. Thus "God put forward [Christ] as an expiation [propitiation] by his blood" (Rom. 3:25); "in him we have redemption through his blood" (Eph. 1:7); "we are now justified by his blood" (Rom. 5:9); and God acted "to reconcile to himself all things, . . . making peace by the blood of his cross" (Col. 1:20).

Stott concludes from the centrality of Christ's blood in these great salvific themes that sacrificial "substitution is not a 'theory of the atonement.' Nor is it even an additional image to take its place as an option alongside the others. It is rather the essence of each image and the heart of the atonement itself." None of the other images "could stand without it."[46]

In the past two chapters we have been examining ideas relating to the saving work of Christ. We will now turn to His life itself to look at what He accomplished for us.

---

[1] Stott, *Cross of Christ*, p. 168. See also the closing "perspective" to the present chapter.

[2] Octavius Winslow, *No Condemnation in Christ Jesus* (London, 1857), p. 358, quoted in John Murray, *The Epistle to the Romans*, New International Commentary on the New Testament (Grand Rapids: Eerdmans, 1959, 1965), vol. 1, p. 324.

[3] A. G. Hebert, "Atone, Atonement," in *A Theological Word Book of the Bible*, ed. Allan Richardson, p. 25; Friedrich Büchsel, "*Hilasmos* and *Katharmos* in the Greek World," in *Theological Dictionary of the New Testament*, ed. G. Kittel and G. Friedrich, vol. 3, pp. 310, 311.

[4] Leon Morris, *The Apostolic Preaching of the Cross* (Grand Rapids: Eerdmans, 1955), p. 161. (Italics supplied.)

[5] Morris, *The Atonement*, p. 157.

[6] William Sanday and Arthur C. Headlam, *The Epistle to the Romans*, 5th ed., International Critical Commentary (Edinburgh: T. & T. Clark, 1902), p. 91.

[7] See Richardson, *Theology of the New Testament*, p. 77; White, *The Desire of Ages*, p. 686: "As man He must suffer the consequences of man's sin. As man He must endure the wrath of God against transgression."

[8] James Denney, *Studies in Theology* (London: Hodder and Stoughton, 1895), p. 108; Forsyth, *Work of Christ*, p. 147. On the concept of a divine penalty for sin, Vincent Taylor has concluded that "it is impossible to think of the suffering of Jesus Himself as anything else but penal suffering. . . . Jesus entered into the blight and judgment which rests upon sin, and bore its shame and desolation upon His heart" (*Jesus and His Sacrifice*, pp. 289, 290). In another connection, Taylor noted that "penal" has some misleading connotations, but that "unfortunately, for the purposes of theology, no good alternative has been suggested" (*The Cross of Christ* [London: Macmillan, 1956], p. 94); cf. Denney, *Christian Doctrine of Reconciliation*, p. 273.

[9] James Denney, *The Death of Christ*, rev. and enl. ed. (New York: George H. Doran, n.d.), p. 127; Dale, *The Atonement*, p. liv.

[10] Denney, *Studies in Theology*, pp. 103, 104; McDonald, *Atonement of the Death of Christ*, p. 24; Ellen White, *Review and Herald*, Apr. 23, 1901, p. 257.

[11] Edward Hepenstall, "Subjective and Objective Aspects of the Atonement," in *The Sanctuary and the Atonement*, ed. Wallekampf and Lesher, p. 687.

[12] Denney, *Death of Christ*, p. 119.

[13] C.E.B. Cranfield, *The Epistle to the Romans*, International Critical Commentary (Edinburgh: T. & T. Clark, 1975, 1979), vol. 1, pp. 199, 217, 216.

[14] White, *Steps to Christ*, p. 13; italics supplied; Forsyth, *Cruciality of the Cross*, p. 41. Cf. Büchsel, "*Hilasmos* and *Katharmos*," vol. 3, p. 322.

[15] Heppenstall, "Subjective and Objective Aspects of the Atonement," p. 682.

The Cross of Christ

[16] Berkouwer, *Sin*, p. 355; Heppenstall, "Subjective and Objective Aspects of the Atonement," p. 679.

[17] Ellen G. White, *Christ's Object Lessons* (Washington, D.C.: Review and Herald, 1900), pp. 128, 129.

[18] Morris, *The Atonement*, pp. 107, 108.

[19] Ellen G. White, *Selected Messages* (Washington, D.C.: Review and Herald, 1958), book 1, p. 309.

[20] See Gustaf Aulén, *Christus Victor* (New York: Macmillan, 1966), pp. 52, 53.

[21] Morris, *The Atonement*, pp. 129, 130. Cf. Brunner, *The Mediator*, p. 521.

[22] Norman R. Gulley, *Christ Our Substitute* (Washington, D.C.: Review and Herald, 1982), p. 23.

[23] Vincent Taylor, *Forgiveness and Reconciliation*, 2nd ed. (London: Macmillan, 1948), p. 68. In spite of our focusing on a *theological concept* of justification in this chapter, we should also realize that the *word* "justification" has more than one meaning in the New Testament. See, e.g., James 2:21, 25.

[24] George Eldon Ladd, *A Theology of the New Testament* (Grand Rapids: Eerdmans, 1974), pp. 437, 443, 445, 446.

[25] Morris, *The Atonement*, p. 195.

[26] Cranfield, *Romans*, vol. 1, p. 212.

[27] D. M. Lloyd-Jones, *Romans: An Exposition of Chapters 3.20-4.25: Atonement and Justification* (Grand Rapids: Zondervan, 1971), pp. 106-108.

[28] John R. W. Stott, *The Letters of John*, rev. ed., Tyndale New Testament Commentaries (Grand Rapids: Eerdmans, 1988), p. 83.

[29] Colin G. Kruse, *The Letters of John*, The Pillar New Testament Commentary (Grand Rapids: Eerdmans, 2000), p. 70.

[30] Brunner, *The Mediator*, p. 462.

[31] Karl Barth, *Church Dogmatics*, trans. G. W. Bromiley (New York: Charles Scribner's Sons, 1956), vol. 4, part 1, p. 22.

[32] See Walker, *Gospel of Reconciliation*, pp. 15-31; Heppenstall, *Our High Priest*, pp. 25-32.

[33] Sanday and Headlam, *Romans*, p. 130.

[34] Forsyth, *Work of Christ*, pp. 80-82, 57, 58.

[35] Taylor, *Atonement in New Testament Teaching*, p. 193; Taylor, *Forgiveness and Reconciliation*, p. xiii.

[36] Walker, *Gospel of Reconciliation*, pp. 196, 197.

[37] Taylor, *Forgiveness and Reconciliation*, p. 93.

[38] Johnsson, *In Absolute Confidence*, p. 101.

[39] William G. Johnsson, "Defilement/Purification and Hebrews 9:23," in *Issues in the Book of Hebrews*, ed. Frank B. Holbrook (Silver Spring, Md.: Biblical Research Institute, General Conference of Seventh-day Adventists, 1989), pp. 91, 87. See also William G. Johnsson, "Defilement and Purification in the Book of Hebrews" (Ph.D. diss. Vanderbilt University, 1973).

[40] Johnsson, "Defilement/Purification," p. 92.

[41] *Ibid.*, p. 98.

[42] William L. Lane, *Hebrews 9-13*, Word Biblical Commentary (Dallas: Word Books, 1991), p. 247.

[43] Craig R. Koester, *Hebrews*, The Anchor Bible (New York: Doubleday, 2001), p. 427.

[44] Stott, *Cross of Christ*, pp. 202, 203.

[45] *Ibid.*, p. 202; Rice, *Reign of God*, p. 177.

[46] Stott, *Cross of Christ*, pp. 202, 203.

Chapter 5

Jesus' Real Temptation and the "Godforsakenness" of the Cross

When evangelical Christians speak of the atonement, they nearly always mean the cross and generally the Resurrection. Protestant liberals in relation to the atonement tend to emphasize Christ's incarnation, teachings, and exemplary life. But when Seventh-day Adventists refer to the atonement, they have often meant Christ's heavenly ministry in the antitypical day of atonement. Who is right—the evangelicals, the Protestant liberals, or the Adventists?

The answer is kind of like asking which part is most important to a smooth-running car—the engine, the wheels, or the steering mechanism. One might argue that it is the engine, since you couldn't possibly have a successful automobile without an engine. Of course, another might claim that your special, all-important engine wouldn't get very far without wheels. The truth is that it takes all the basic parts to make a functional automobile.

The work of Christ in the plan of salvation is like that. All aspects of Christ's life, ministry, and death are important. For example, there would have been no cross without the Incarnation and sinless life, no Resurrection without the cross, and no heavenly ministry without all three. And even all those put together, as we shall see in this chapter and the next, are not the entire atonement. The atonement as seen in Christ's work is not a point—it is more like a line. Thus it is not something that merely happened at the cross, but is rather something that began when sin entered the universe, and will not be completed until the final destruction of sin in the lake of fire (Rev. 20:10, 14, 15). While Christ's cross was climactic in the process of atonement, it was but one step in God's saving work.

Vincent Taylor said it nicely: "It is not alone by His death that Christ brings us to God; it is also by His life, resurrection and present mediatorial ministry on high. [However,] Calvary is the focal point of that ministry in terms of history; it is the place where we see God in the plenitude of His reconciling love." The atonement, Taylor emphasizes, is "the whole process by which sinners are reconciled to God."[1]

With that fact in mind, the present chapter will examine the theological significance of several stages of Christ's work.

Christ's Self-emptying

The first point to note regarding Christ's defeat of Satan is Christ's identity. One of the most interesting (and controversial) texts on the topic is Philippians 2:5-8: "Have this mind among yourselves, which is yours in Christ Jesus, who, *though he was in the form of God*, did not count equality with God a thing to be grasped, but *emptied himself, taking the form of a servant, being born in the likeness of men*. And being found in human form he humbled himself and became obedient unto death, even death on a cross."

Our passage tells us that Jesus was "in the form of God." Christ never had the form of God in the sense of mere outward appearance, but in that of possessing "the essential characteristics and attributes of God."[2] In fact, we learn from other passages that Jesus was not just like God—He was God (John 1:1, 14). He was neither human nor an angel, but the Godhead's agent in creation of both the universe and its moral structure (John 1:3; Col. 1:16; Heb. 1:2).

Paul tells us that Christ, despite His divinity, came to earth "taking the form [essential attributes and characteristics] of a servant" (Phil. 2:7). Christ did not come as superior to other humans, but like them. One of the great mysteries of the universe is that Jesus Christ was both divine and human at the same time.

It is beyond the grasp of human intelligence to understand fully the meaning of what Philippians 2 tells us Christ did, but certain points do seem clear from the text. One is that Christ's incarnation was a crucial part of His mission, since while "found in human form he humbled himself and became obedient unto death, even death on a cross" (verse 8).

A second thing we can understand from verses 5-8 is that Christ "emptied himself" of something when He became a human being. While the apostle does not define his exact meaning, it seems clear from a study of the rest of the New Testament that part of what Christ did in becoming human was to strip Himself voluntarily "of the insignia and prerogatives of deity." Thus Paul seems to be saying that "Christ voluntarily gave up . . . his divine attributes and submitted to all the conditions of human life."[3]

In other words, Jesus remained God, but voluntarily chose not to use

Jesus' Real Temptation and the "Godforsakenness" of the Cross

His divine powers on His own behalf. Jesus did not give up His divinity. Rather, He chose not to use it. While on earth, God the Son lived in dependence upon God the Father, as did other people (John 5:19, 30; 8:28; 14:10). He did not come to earth to live as God, but to live in obedience to God as a human being and to overcome where Adam and Eve fell (Rom. 5:15-19; Phil. 2:8).

As Ellen White put it: "The power of the Saviour's Godhead was hidden. He overcame in human nature, relying upon God for power." She went on to add that we can have that same privilege.[4]

The New Testament appears to indicate that the disciples did have the same power through the Holy Spirit that Jesus possessed to heal, exorcise demons, and even resurrect the dead (see Mark 6:7-13; Luke 9:1-6; Acts 9:33-41; 14:8-10; 20:9, 10).

The crucial thing to notice at this point is that Christ "emptied himself" of His divine prerogatives. No one else "emptied" Him. His was a *voluntary* act. As a result, He could resume His divine powers at any moment He chose to do so. The significance of this is that, unlike any other human being, Jesus could have used His awesome powers as God at a split second. To do so, however, would have broken the plan of salvation, in which Jesus came to disprove Satan's claim that no person could keep God's law. Jesus came as a human being to live in obedience, even unto "death on a cross" (Phil. 2:8).

It was at the point of Christ's voluntary self-emptying that we find the focus and strength of His temptations throughout His life and at His death. Having "humbled himself," He became, as Taylor points out, "the Unknown whom men might deride, the Stranger on whom they might spit."[5] If the enemy just had been able to get Jesus to "un-empty" Himself one time and cause Him to employ His "hidden" power, the war would have been over. If Satan could have tempted Christ to use His divinity in anger or on His own behalf, he would have triumphed over the Savior.

Christ's voluntary self-emptying lay at the foundation of His temptations. He was not merely tempted as we are, but He was tempted far beyond the point where ordinary humans can ever be, since He actually had the power of God "in" (rather than "at") His fingertips.

The great struggle of Christ was to stay emptied. Satan's forceful temptations were to get Him to "un-empty." Thus, writes W. M. Clow, "Christ hung upon His cross from His cradle to His grave." His was a total life of self-denial and self-crucifixion. "When you think of the self-emptying which brought Christ to earth," P. T. Forsyth penned, "His whole life was a living death." "It was as difficult for him," Ellen White suggests, "to keep [to] the level of humanity as it is for men to rise above the low level of their depraved natures, and be partakers of the divine nature."[6]

For His entire life, Jesus faced the constant temptation to "un-empty" Himself. His was to be a life of surrendered obedience, "*even* [unto] death on a cross." That death and all it entailed, as we shall see, was the toughest part of His assignment.

Overcoming Where Adam Failed

If we see the Incarnation as a first step in Christ's victory, then we should view His perfect life of obedience as a second. Part of what Christ came to accomplish was to demonstrate that Satan's claim that God's law could not be kept was a falsehood.[7]

Adam, unfortunately, had failed at that very point. As a result, "many died through one man's trespass," but "by one man's obedience many will be made righteous" (Rom. 5:15, 19). Christ, as the "second Adam," came to succeed where the first Adam had fallen short.

The New Testament presents Christ's life as a moral achievement. Despite entering the world with the physical results of sin, He overcame Satan's every assault. Thus, John Murray writes, "the Scripture regards the work of Christ as one of obedience."[8]

Christ said in the midst of His ministry that "I have come down from heaven, not to do my own will, but the will of him who sent me" (John 6:38). And at the end of His work Jesus could say, "I have kept my Father's commandments and abide in his love" (John 15:10). As a result, He claimed, "the ruler of this world" had "no power" over Him (John 14:30).

"If," John Stott asserts, "he had disobeyed, by deviating an inch from the path of God's will, the devil would have gained a toehold and frustrated the plan of salvation." In Jesus' life, Ellen White pens, "the principles of God's law—love to God and man—were perfectly exemplified. Benevolence, unselfish love, was the life of His soul."[9] Christ was tempted "in every respect" that we are, "yet without sin" (Heb. 4:15).

Unlike every other human being, Christ did not fall short in obedience (Rom. 3:23). As the second Adam He won the victory for God and for those who believe in Him. Christ's victorious life made the cross meaningful. Without a victorious life there could not have been a victorious death. Satan had no right to take, of all earthlings, Christ's life, because our Lord had not sinned.

Meanwhile, Christ as a human did not have it easy. Satan sought to

Jesus' Real Temptation and the "Godforsakenness" of the Cross

destroy Him from His very birth and thereby cancel His mission (Matt. 2:1-18; Rev. 12:4). One of the most remarkable things that we find throughout the Gospels is the large amount of demonic activity. Satan and his agents are more in evidence in the Gospels than anywhere else in the Bible. "This is not accidental," Michael Green claims. "If Jesus Christ came primarily to destroy the works of the devil, if his arrival on the scene was the signal for the final battle to begin, then it is not so surprising that Satan should be stirred" to activity.[10]

The Bible tells us that immediately after Christ's baptism, He experienced His wilderness temptations.

According to Matthew, the first temptation involved commanding "stones to become loaves of bread" (Matt. 4:3, 4). I used to think that that was a foolish temptation. After all, I could go out behind my house to try to turn rocks into bread all year and never have a loaf for dinner. It is no temptation to me because I can't make bread out of rocks, and I know it. But—and here is the point—Jesus could. As the agent of creation of all that exists, He could produce bread out of nothing. Some circles engage in a great deal of discussion regarding what it meant for Jesus to be tempted "in every respect . . . as we are, yet without sin" (Heb. 4:15). It seems from a simple reading of the Bible that Jesus, irrespective of the constitution of His human nature, faced temptations far beyond that which any other person can ever experience. Most of His temptations could never attract us because we lack the ability to respond to them successfully.

Christ had been without food for more than a month when Satan urged him to create bread. Certainly it must have been an attractive suggestion, but we miss the point if we see it merely as a desire to satisfy His appetite. The real temptation was to reverse the self-emptying of Philippians 2 by using His divine power to meet His personal needs.[11] That, of course, would mean that He was not facing the world like other people. Underlying the temptation was the subtle insinuation that He could, if He were truly God, use His special powers for Himself. Beyond that, as we shall see shortly, transforming stones into bread in a land like Palestine—full of both hunger and rocks—hinted at the possibility of establishing a kingdom by a more attractive way than death on a cross.

We might think of the second temptation in Matthew's list as a public leap to fame (Matt. 4:5-7). Taking Jesus to the pinnacle of the Jerusalem Temple, Satan, quoting Scripture as he did in Eden, suggests that Jesus could prove His divinity by jumping into the milling throng below.

Absurd as it may seem to us, that wasn't a bad idea. After all, weren't

The Cross of Christ

the Jews always looking for a "sign" (1 Cor. 1:22; Matt. 12:38) by which to identify the Messiah? Here was the perfect example. A leap from the top of the Temple, towering 400 feet above the Valley of Hinnom below, would be impressive indeed. "Would not," suggests John Yoder, "an unexpected apparition from above have been the most self-evident way for the messenger of the covenant, in the words of Malachi (3:1-4), to come 'suddenly to his temple' to 'purify the sons of Levi'?"[12]

Nothing impressed Jews more than fulfilling Bible prophecy. The people would easily line up behind that type of Messiah—it was what they wanted. The public Temple jump was a temptation precisely because it would be a more popular and painless way to win a following than a crucifixion. Its results would have been immediate.

The third temptation hit Jesus at the level of human ambition. The "prince of this world" promised Christ the world's political power if He would only follow his satanic program (Matt. 4:8-10). If Christ merely would accept Satan's values, all would be His. Christ could have all the kingdoms of the world if He only would give His allegiance to the tempter. The point to remember is that the offer of world dominion was in line with the main themes of Old Testament Messianic prophecy. Did not the prophets teach that all nations would flow to Jerusalem and that "all nations shall gather to it"? (Isa. 2:2; Jer. 3:17). World dominion was a Messianic function.

The people of Israel were ready for a political Messiah. The whole nation seethed with hatred against Rome, the invader and oppressor. "If He led a revolt," Leslie Weatherhead wrote, "a thousand swords would flash from their uneasy scabbards."[13] The Jews were expecting a political Messiah. If only Jesus would have taken that track, most of the nation would have followed Him. Certainly, the temptation ran, there have to be more successful roads to Messiahship than the way of the cross.

The third temptation, then, represented a shortcut to world dominion. Raoul Dederen has correctly written that Christ's special temptation throughout His life was "to depart from the accomplishment of His mission as Redeemer and turn from the path of suffering and death that His Messianic mission necessarily entailed."[14]

All Christ's temptations, we should note, centered on having Him give up His dependency on the Father—to take control of His own life by becoming "un-emptied." They were all aimed at distracting Him from absolute obedience, especially from being "obedient unto death, even death on a cross" (Phil. 2:8).

Jesus' Real Temptation and the "Godforsakenness" of the Cross

==The temptation in the wilderness represents a microcosm of Christ's temptations throughout His life==. The themes of the wilderness temptation reappeared periodically. The one concerning "bread," for example, emerges several times in the Gospels. One of those occasions occurred when Jesus fed the 5,000. That miracle deeply impressed the Jews. "When the people saw the sign which he had done," John notes, "they said, 'This is indeed the prophet who is to come into the world!'" Then followed a move on the part of the Jews to "take him by force to make him king" (John 6:14, 15).

The people identified Christ as "the prophet who is to come" because of His powerful "sign." Josephus (c. A.D. 37-c. A.D. 100) tells us that in nearly every case the themes of "the prophet" and the working of signs accompanied Jewish first-century political uprisings by would-be liberators.[15] Building on the Messianic promise that God would "raise up . . . a prophet" like Moses (Deut. 18:18), the Jews at the feeding of the 5,000 thought that they were experiencing a fulfillment of prophecy.

The connection they made was that Moses, the great deliverer, gave their "fathers . . . manna in the wilderness" (John 6:31). Now they had someone who appeared to be a second Moses. Jesus was a second deliverer—another prophet, who like Moses could supply bread from heaven. Thus the attempt to make Him king. The disciples even got carried away with the possibility. Matthew tells us that Jesus had to "make" them get into the boat and start their homeward journey, while He dismissed the crowds (Matt. 14:22). The disciples saw the Messianic potential clearly. *Now*, they must have thought, *is the time for Jesus to make His master stroke.*

For Jesus, however, it was the ultimate temptation. He could indeed create bread out of "stones," and the people had been impressed—so impressed that they were ready to set up His kingdom on the spot. Even Christ's "support group" was behind the movement. Here was temptation of the first order. "Build the Kingdom," the temptation runs, "on bread. Make it the first point of your program to abolish hunger. Multiply loaves and fishes all the time," and the people will love you.[16]

Again we find the old lure of establishing His kingdom without a cross, without having to follow the path of a rejected servant. We see the seriousness of the episode reflected by the fact that immediately after dismissing the crowds, "he went up on the mountain by himself to pray" (Matt. 14:23; John 6:15). He needed to commit Himself anew to the accomplishment of God's will, and to pray especially for His disciples, who desired a Messiah out of harmony with that will. The doing of God's will in the accomplishment of His mission must remain central in His life. That is always a matter of prayer.

An even more forceful exhibition of the problem of Jesus' temptation "to avoid" the consequences of His mission appears in Matthew 16. At Caesarea Philippi Jesus sought to discover who His disciples really thought He was. After several false starts, Peter finally suggested that Jesus was "the Christ" ("Messiah" in Hebrew; verse 16).

Jesus commended Peter for the answer, noting that recognition of His divine Messiahship would be the foundation of His church (verse 18). The problem was that although the disciples had believed that Jesus was God's Messiah, they had still not understood what that fact represented. "To them," William Barclay writes, "it meant something totally different from what it meant to Jesus. They were still thinking in terms of a conquering Messiah, a warrior king, who would sweep the Romans from Palestine and lead Israel to power."[17]

So Jesus began to explain to the disciples that, rejected by the Jewish leaders, He would "be killed, and on the third day be raised" (verse 21). That answer was too much for Peter, who still envisioned himself as a kind of prime minister or first vice president in the new kingdom. The disciple blurted out that Christ did not have to die. At that point, Jesus gave one of the sharpest rebukes of His entire recorded ministry. To Peter He said: "Get behind me, Satan! You are a hindrance to me; for you are not on the side of God, but of men" (verses 22, 23).

Jesus reacted so forcefully because of the magnitude of the problem. He had seen crucifixions in His travels and, like any normal human being, had no desire to exit from the world on a cross. Beyond that, every person loves acceptance. We get a sense of well-being from having people think good of us in our success. Thus Jesus, as the Gospels picture Him, was like us. He had no hankering for either human rejection or death on a cross. But the issue of Christ's cross, as we shall shortly see, involved more than mere death or human rejection—and that more would make the circumstances of His death especially loathsome to Him. Satan had tempted Him all along with an easier way. And here was one of Christ's most trusted disciples playing Satan's role as tempter.

The cross was central to the great struggle between Christ and Satan. Jesus could have become a political messiah through feeding the people and leading a rebellion against the Romans, but He would not have been God's Christ, the Savior of the world. Because of that, Jesus firmly rejected Peter's suggestion, knowing that without the cross there would be no sal-

Jesus' Real Temptation and the "Godforsakenness" of the Cross

vation. As we noted in chapters 3 and 4, Jesus never downplayed the centrality of the cross and His sacrificial death. It was the foundation of His mission, even if it was unpleasant.

"If Jesus had done as Peter suggested," Michael Green writes, "there would have been no cross, no redemption, and the ploy of the tempter back in the wilderness would eventually have come off, as the old serpent tried once again, this time through the agency of a trusted friend and colleague." Peter, to put it bluntly, "had been deceived by the devil to deny the necessity of the cross."[18]

The Death of Temptation

The triumphal entry of Jesus into Jerusalem created an aura of expectation. The people felt it, the rulers sensed it, the disciples excitedly anticipated it, and Jesus dreaded it. "Now is my soul troubled," He said shortly before the Last Supper. He questioned to Himself whether He should ask the Father to save Him from the "hour" coming upon Him. "No," He concluded, "for this purpose I have come to this hour." Then, in response to His prayer, God's voice came from heaven, assuring Jesus that He was on the right path (John 12:27, 28). In that emotionally high state of assurance, Jesus gave the people a clear statement of the meaning of what would transpire in the next few days.

"*Now,*" He claimed, "*is the judgment of this world, now shall the ruler of this world be cast out; and I, when I am lifted up from the earth [on the cross], will draw all men to myself.*" The crowd, however, was not impressed. The people inquired how He could be crucified if He were really the Messiah, since they had heard from Scripture that "the Christ remains for ever" (verses 31-34).

In spite of the Father's assurance, as Jesus approached His cross a sense of dread began to overcome Him. The apex of His struggle with temptation took place in Gethsemane as He came face to face with the horror of what the cross really meant.

Mark presents Jesus in Gethsemane as "greatly distressed and troubled," saying to the disciples: "My soul is very sorrowful, even to death" (Mark 14:33, 34; compare Matt. 26:37, 38). Next, leaving James, John, and Peter behind, He "fell on his face and prayed," asking that "if it were possible, the hour might pass from" Him. He then, noting that all things are possible with the Father, prayed: "Remove this cup from me." Returning twice to His sleeping disciples, Jesus went away both times to repeat essentially the same prayer (see Matt. 26:36-46; Mark 14:32-42; Luke 22:39-46).

The Cross of Christ

One thing is clear from this experience: Jesus dreaded both His "hour" and His "cup." Several writers have recognized a sharp contrast between Christ's fear of His impending death and the reaction of other famous martyrs down through history.

Many have faced death calmly. Socrates of fifth-century Athens, for instance, is often cited as an example of the way a wise man faces the termination of his earthly life. For Socrates, writes Oscar Cullmann, "death is the soul's great friend." Socrates had "proved" to his satisfaction a theory of the immortality of the soul. Thus he had nothing to fear from death, the liberator of his being.

On the day of his death, the great teacher traced the arguments for immortality for his students. Then, to demonstrate his faith, Socrates calmly took the poison hemlock (as dictated by the court) and cheerfully drank it down. "At that moment," Cullmann pens, "he lived this doctrine. . . . Socrates goes to his death in complete peace and composure. The death of Socrates is a beautiful death. Nothing is seen here of death's terror. . . . Whoever fears death," from Socrates' viewpoint, "proves that he loves the world of the body."[19]

Christian martyrs have also faced death serenely, and even ecstatically at times. For example, when Polycarp (c. A.D. 69-c. A.D. 155), the second-century bishop of Smyrna, stood before the proconsul who would soon take his life, he told his persecutor to get on with the job. A letter written soon after his martyrdom in A.D. 155 or 156 tells us that approaching his death, "he was inspired with courage and joy, and his face was filled with grace, so that not only did he not collapse in fright at the things which were said to him," but he expressed a joyful reaction.[20]

Such has been the experience of many martyrs down through history. Knowing they are right with God, they have no fear of death.

With so many joyful deaths evident in history, one must ask why Christ so fearfully anticipated His. Did He love this world too much? Did He lack faith? Or was He just plain scared of pain?

The answer seems to lie in another direction. It had to do with the nature of the "cup" He had to drink and the significance of the "hour" He had to experience. Drinking the "cup of horror and desolation" and the "cup of [God's] wrath" were Old Testament symbols (Eze. 23:33, 34; Isa. 51:17). Christ's cup, John Stott points out, "symbolized neither the physical pain of being flogged and crucified, nor the mental distress of being despised and rejected . . . , but rather the spiritual agony of bearing the sins of the world, in other words, of enduring the divine judgment which those sins deserved."[21]

The book of Revelation would later use the drinking of the cup of God's wrath in referring to those who had rejected Christ (Rev. 14:10; 18:6). All human beings, as we noted earlier, are under God's wrath (that is, His anger with and judgment of sin). Christ drank the cup of judgment for all, but what He did becomes effective for them only as they accept His sacrifice by faith. Those who reject Christ are choosing to drink their own cup in the Lamb's judgment day (John 3:36; Rev. 6:15-17; Rom. 5:1, 9, 10).

Christ's dread in Gethsemane stemmed from His realization of God's hatred of sin. It was almost unbearable that He must become "a curse for us" and become "sin" in God's eyes (Gal. 3:13; 2 Cor. 5:21). "He felt that by sin," Ellen White penned, "He was being separated from His Father. The gulf was so broad, so black, so deep, that His spirit shuddered before it. This agony He must not exert His divine power to escape. As man He must suffer the consequences of man's sin. As man He must endure the wrath of God against transgression."[22]

In Gethsemane the moment of decision had come. He either had to continue toward the cross or give up His mission. The tempter, of course, was still at His side, pointing out that His closest friends couldn't even stay awake to support Him, that one of His disciples was at that very moment on a mission to betray Him, and that the ungrateful people He was dying for would soon demand His crucifixion.

Fighting the temptation to do His own will and back off from the cross, Christ underwent duress that we can grasp only faintly. In great agony and dread Jesus finally made His decision. "My Father," He repeatedly prayed, "if this cannot pass unless I drink it, thy will be done" (Matt. 26:42).

Having set His feet on the road to the cross, Jesus, exuding a calmness missing throughout His Gethsemane experience, went back to the disciples. He had chosen to put temptation to death, His unique temptation to avoid bearing God-separating sin on the cross. The decision to go ahead with His mission irrevocably made, Christ awakened the disciples, announcing to them that "the hour is at hand, and the Son of man is betrayed into the hands of sinners. Rise, let us be going; see, my betrayer is at hand" (Matt. 26:45, 46). When Christ left Gethsemane, He was not looking backward at a fulfilled mission as a perfect example and a great teacher. Rather, He was facing forward to the climactic point of His mission, which He was soon to experience.

It Is Finished

The life of Christ demonstrated that God was right and Satan wrong. God's law of love could be perfectly kept. But His life was only a partial

The Cross of Christ

illustration of the issues in the conflict between God and Satan. The decisive display of the results of the two opposing sets of principles took place at the Crucifixion.

Crucifixion, as we noted in chapter 3, was an agonizing death. With its helpless public nakedness, physical pain, maddening thirst, and public shame it was a hideous way to die. However, many thousands had perished in that manner by the time of Christ's death, and thousands more would be crucified in subsequent decades. Yet none of their deaths made a difference in world history. What, we find ourselves forced to ask, was so special about Christ's crucifixion?

It was not the form of His death that was important, but who it was that died. Jesus was not just another human being, but the sinless Son of God, who partook of human nature "that through death he might destroy him who has the power of death, that is, the devil" (Heb. 2:14). Christ, as we noted earlier, "emptied himself" by taking human form and becoming "obedient unto death, even death on a cross" (Phil. 2:5-8).

A major difference between Christ's crucifixion and that of others is that Christ did not have to stay on the cross. As D. M. Baillie put it, "Jesus did not die as a helpless victim: He could have escaped."[23] As the man who was God He could have "un-emptied" Himself, snapped the bonds that held Him, and ended the ordeal.

The point is, however, that Jesus had *chosen* to die on the cross. His crucifixion was a voluntary act of obedience to God's will. "The good shepherd lays down his life for the sheep," He had earlier told His hearers. Again He said: "I lay down my life. . . . No one takes it from me, but I lay it down of my own accord" (John 10:11, 17, 18). Thus Christ *could* have come down from the cross, but He *would* not.

While Jesus hung on the cross, the tempter still sought to get Him to "un-empty" Himself; this time in the person of those He was dying for. Passersby "derided him," crying out that He had made great statements about what He could do. If you are who you claim to be, they challenged, "save yourself, and come down from the cross!" The chief priests and scribes also got into the action, mocking Him to one another and saying: "He saved others; he cannot save himself. Let the Christ, the King of Israel, come down now from the cross, that we may see and believe." They were still after a "sign." Meanwhile, some of the Roman guard "also mocked him" (Mark 15:29-32; Luke 23:36).

How would you have responded to such challenges and treatment? I tell you how I would have most likely reacted. I would have called down fire from heaven and "zapped 'em" with a "slow sizzle" so that such ungratefuls could suffer a bit and think about who I was before they died. They would certainly be sorry that they had exhausted my patience when I was trying so hard to do them a favor. I would give them exactly what they deserved!

Now, Christ could have done that. He could have summoned "more than twelve legions of angels" (Matt. 26:53) to His rescue and laid the countryside waste. Or He could have met force with force, but the cost would have been the "un-emptying" of Himself and the forfeiture of the plan of salvation. Instead He prayed, saying: "Father, forgive them; for they know not what they do" (Luke 23:34). In other words, Jesus gave them what they did not deserve—grace.

One of the interesting sidelights of the Synoptic Gospel accounts of the Crucifixion is that they provide us with no details dealing with such things as hammers, nails, pain, or even blood. On the other hand, the evangelists are quite concerned with Jesus' attitudes and spiritual agony on the cross.

Of special import is Christ's cry of dereliction: "My God, my God, why hast thou forsaken me?" (Mark 15:34). It expresses, as we have seen, a very different attitude from that of others who had died with full assurance that all would be well. The final words of Dietrich Bonhoeffer, Christian underground leader against Hitler, to his friend as he went to his execution were: "'This is the end—for me the beginning of life.'"[24] Such were the words of a man of faith.

Some have viewed the passion and death of Christ as a "consummation of his unity with the father" rather than a bearing of God's judgment on sin.[25] Such individuals generally see Christ's death as a demonstration of God's love for sinners rather than primarily a judgment on sin. That interpretation not only reads a great deal into the plain words of Christ, but overlooks large numbers of texts to the contrary throughout the rest of the Bible that regard Christ's substitutionary sacrifice for sin as the foundation of the plan of salvation.[26]

Christ did die a martyr's death, but martyrdom did not exhaust His mission. A martyred Messiah, P. T. Forsyth writes, "could impress but not forgive; he could move men but not redeem them; he could criticize [sic] society but not judge the world."[27]

The significance of Christ is not that He was a moral hero. His agony on the cross was because He was bearing the sins of the world and God's judgment on sin (2 Cor. 5:21; Gal. 3:13; Heb. 10:9-14).[28] "Plenty of men,"

The Cross of Christ

Forsyth penned, "can be obedient unto death; but the core of Christianity is Christ's being obedient unto judgment, and unto the final judgment of holiness."[29]

Christ did not utter His cry of forsakenness until He had become sin for us upon the cross. For the first time in His life the relationship between Him and the Father appeared to be broken. "The Saviour," Ellen White wrote, "could not see through the portals of the tomb. Hope did not present to Him His coming forth from the grave a conqueror, or tell Him of the Father's acceptance of the sacrifice. He feared that sin was so offensive to God that Their separation was to be eternal. Christ felt the anguish which the sinner will feel when mercy shall no longer plead for the guilty race."[30]

The reason for the contrast between Jesus' death and those of Bonhoeffer and Polycarp was that they were experiencing physical death, whereas He was also enduring the spiritual separation from God stemming from divine judgment on sin (wrath). Augustine (354-430) highlighted that when he described Christ's death as a "double death" for us.[31]

Thus it was that the Savior, who was ushered into the world with brightness at midnight, died in the midst of darkness at noon (Mark 15:33). "As a 'blasphemer,'" Jürgen Moltmann observes, "Jesus was rejected by the guardians of his people's law. As a 'rebel' he was crucified by the Romans. But finally, and most profoundly," he died as one apparently "rejected by his God and his Father." It is the theological meaning of Christ's death, Moltmann adds, that alone "distinguishes his cross from the many crosses of forgotten and nameless persons in world history."[32]

It was not the pain, disgrace, or human rejection that brought about the death of Jesus. Rather, Ellen White declares, "it was the burden of sin, the sense of its terrible enormity, of its separation of the soul from God—it was this that broke the heart of the Son of God." Forsyth has meaningfully concluded that "you do not understand Christ till you understand His cross."[33]

"The greatest single word ever uttered"[34] was undoubtedly Christ's just before His death: "It is finished" (John 19:30; one word in Greek). He then committed His spirit to the Father's hands and died (Luke 23:46). The three Synoptic Gospels do not tell us that Jesus said "It is finished," but they all indicate that Jesus died with a great shout upon His lips (Matt. 27:50; Mark 15:37; Luke 23:46). Thus it would appear that Jesus died with a shout of triumph. "He did not say," writes Barclay, "'It is finished,' in weary defeat; He said it as one who shouts for joy because the victory is won."[35]

At the time of Christ's death "the curtain of the temple was torn in two, from top to bottom" (Matt. 27:51), signifying that the atonement for sin was now complete and that, therefore, the Jewish sacrificial services had come to an end.³⁶ The great sacrifice of Christ that the Levitical services had pointed forward to had come, and the old system was now obsolete.

Christ's death on the cross sealed Satan's defeat. The devil had demonstrated his malice in killing the sinless Son of God. Satan had a right to the lives of other people because through sin they had brought the death penalty onto themselves, but Jesus stood in a class by Himself. He had not sinned. As a result, Satan had "no power" or authority over Him (John 14:30). While Satan had hoped to the end that Jesus would "un-empty" Himself, take up His divine power, and forfeit the plan of salvation, Christ had held firm to the Father's will.

The cross demonstrated two things—God's love and justice, and Satan's hate and deceptiveness concerning God's character. R. J. Campbell summed it up nicely when he wrote: "At Calvary perfect love joined issue with perfect hate, perfect goodness with perfect wickedness, and became victorious by enduring the worst and remaining pure and unchanged to the last."³⁷

The love of God in giving His Son and the utter hatred of Satan were both plain to see for the onlooking universe. Beyond that, *all could recognize that God had maintained His holiness and justice in the way He had handled the sin problem. He neglected neither the requirements of the law nor its just penalty. All was accounted for at Calvary. The cross put divine forgiveness on a moral basis.*

"Not until the death of Christ," Ellen White wrote, "was the character of Satan clearly revealed to the angels or to the unfallen worlds. The archapostate had so clothed himself with deception that even holy beings had not understood his principles." But Satan had overreached himself in taking Christ's life. Never again would he be able to deceive the angels and unfallen beings. "The victory gained at His death on Calvary broke forever the accusing power of Satan over the universe and silenced his charges that self-denial was impossible with God." With the crucifixion of Jesus, "the last link of sympathy between Satan and the heavenly world was broken." Furthermore, "the destruction of sin and Satan was forever made certain, . . . and . . . the universe was made eternally secure."³⁸

Calvary was the turning point in cosmic history. In the book of Revelation it is the blood of the Lamb that is the ground of victorious triumph (Rev. 7:9-14; 5:9, 12). At the defeat of Satan on the cross, John envisioned him being "thrown down to the earth" with "his angels" (Rev. 12:9, 10; cf. John 12:31).

The Cross of Christ

But It Is Obviously Not Finished

Yet if there is one thing obvious about Christ's "finished work," it is that it is not finished. Reflecting on this point, Macquarrie asserts that "men are apparently just as much enslaved as ever."[39] Even though Satan has been defeated, he hasn't conceded that fact. Years after the cross, Peter could write that the devil "prowls around like a roaring lion, seeking some one to devour" (1 Peter 5:8). Thus, Colin Gunton claims, we live in "the tension of the 'now but not yet.'" During this period the work of Christ continues, even though in one sense it was finished at Calvary.[40]

Ellen White has suggested that God did not destroy Satan at the time of the Crucifixion because "the angels did not even then understand all that was involved in the great controversy. The principles at stake were to be more fully revealed." In addition, humanity still needed a fuller revelation of "the contrast between the Prince of light and the prince of darkness."[41]

As a result, the work of salvation goes on. Thus Paul can rightly say that having been "reconciled to God by the death of his Son, *much more, now that we are reconciled, shall we be saved by his life*" (Rom. 5:10).

The resurrection of Christ is the key to understanding the New Testament from Acts through Revelation. The disciples did not view Christ's shameful death as a victory. Rather, it was a public defeat and a rejection of His claims. His death destroyed their hopes in Him. If Christ had not been raised, George Eldon Ladd writes, redemptive history and Christianity would have ended in "the *cul-de-sac* of a Palestinian grave."[42] Without the Resurrection, Christianity would have nothing to offer the world except a few nice ideas.

The great transformation of the disciples stands as one of the impressive evidences of the Resurrection.[43] That event, Stalker tells us, transfigured everything. "It changed the terrible series of events through which they [the apostles] had been passing from being the act and triumph of sinful men into the design of the wonder-working God; it changed Jesus from being a false and discredited Messiah into the King of kings and the Lord of lords; and it changed themselves from the shamed adherents of a defeated cause into the champions and witnesses of a gospel" that would spread around the world.[44]

The Resurrection separates Jesus from all other heroes in history. Bonhoeffer is quoted as saying that "Socrates mastered the art of dying," but "Christ overcame death."[45]

The significance of Christ's resurrection lies in its being a validation of His victory on Calvary and an indication of the tangible triumph over

Jesus' Real Temptation and the "Godforsakenness" of the Cross

Satan's stronghold/prison house of death. When Christ arose from the grave, His death became in essence "the death of death." Jesus won the battle by taking on Himself human death and snapping its power. In the Resurrection He dealt with the last enemy—death (1 Cor. 15:26). Unlike the resurrected Lazarus, Jesus did not have to die again. "Christ," Paul wrote, "being raised from the dead will never die again: death no longer has dominion over him" (Rom. 6:9).[46] He had swallowed death up in victory and has pledged to share that victory with His followers (1 Cor. 15:51-56). The resurrected Christ tells His followers: "Fear not, I am the first and the last, and the living one; I died, and behold I am alive for evermore, and I have the keys of Death and Hades" (Rev. 1:17, 18).

It is no wonder that the apostles invariably centered their gospel message on Christ's death and resurrection. The core of their preaching in the book of Acts was "You killed Him, but God raised Him up" (see Acts 2:23, 24; 3:15; 4:10; etc.). The gospel according to Paul was "that Christ died for our sins in accordance with the scriptures, that he was buried, that he was raised on the third day" (1 Cor. 15:1-3). The Resurrection was truly the sign that Christ was the "Son of God in power" (Rom. 1:4).

Christ's post-Resurrection work in heaven helps us gain a broader view of what it means to be "saved by his life" (Rom. 5:10). The Bible presents the risen and victorious Christ as the high priest in the heavenly sanctuary.[47] We read in the book of Hebrews that "we have . . . a high priest, one who is seated at the right hand of the throne of the Majesty in heaven, a minister in the sanctuary and the true tent which is set up not by man but by the Lord." "But when Christ had offered for all time a single sacrifice for sins, he sat down at the right hand of God, then to wait until his enemies should be made a stool for his feet" (Heb. 8:1, 2; 10:12, 13).

Having fulfilled the climactic phase of His atoning work, Christ ascended to heaven to apply the benefits of His earthly accomplishment. That heavenly ministry, Ladd notes, is "one of the central doctrines of the New Testament," but it is "often neglected." "It is by the mediatorial work of the Lord Jesus that every enemy shall be put beneath his feet. When this has been accomplished and he has destroyed 'every rule and every authority and power,' Jesus the Lord will deliver *the kingdom* to God the Father (1 Cor. 15:24)."[48]

"The Christian religion," Denney points out, "depends not on what Christ was, merely, but on what He is; not simply on what He did, but on what He does." The cross does not exhaust the truth of the atoning Christ. H. Wheeler Robinson compared Christ's work on earth to an iceberg. "Just

The Cross of Christ

as the visible part of the iceberg reveals and is part of a greater submerged mass, so the temporal handling of sin is part of the eternal which it reveals."[49]

With those thoughts in mind, it is easy to see why Ellen White claimed that "the intercession of Christ in man's behalf in the sanctuary above is as essential to the plan of salvation as was His death upon the cross. By His death He began that work which after His resurrection He ascended to complete in heaven."[50] The ministration of Christ in the heavenly sanctuary will hold deep significance until the end of the great struggle between Christ and Satan. Both Daniel and John the apostle focus Satan's opposition on God's sanctuary (Dan. 8:11; Rev. 13:6). An attack on the sanctuary is an attack on His throne and thus upon His sovereignty.[51]

The essence of Christ's work in the heavenly sanctuary is the vindication of God and the restoration of humanity. As we noted in chapter 1, those two aspects of His work stand together. We might think of the sanctuary above as the command post in God's war against evil. It is the focal point of His plan of salvation, not only for the Father and the Son, but also for the Holy Spirit and the angels, who are dispatched to work with and in God's children on earth.

While one function of the ministry of the Holy Spirit is to empower Christians to live the Christian life (Gal. 5:16-26; 2:20; Rom. 8:4), Christ recognized that His people would continue to have problems with deeply rooted sin. Even though they had died to sin and had risen to a new way of thinking and acting, the Lord knew that not all of their difficulties had been solved (Rom. 6:1-11; 7:15).

Because God foresaw the problem, He made provision to meet it in the heavenly ministry of Christ. Thus John can say: "I am writing this to you so that you may not sin; but if any one does sin, we have an advocate with the Father, Jesus Christ the righteous." John goes on to assert that Christ has a right to ask for forgiveness for His followers because "he is the expiation [propitiation] for our sins" (1 John 2:1, 2). Jesus removed the barrier between God and sinners, as we saw in chapter 4, by His atoning sacrifice.[52] John, therefore, presents the same basic theme that Paul did in Romans 3:25: God can forgive through Christ because of His atoning sacrifice (propitiation).

"Let us then with confidence draw near to the throne of grace," we read in Hebrews, "that we may receive mercy and find grace [undeserved favor] to help in time of need." Christ "is able for all time to save those who draw near to God through him, since he always lives to make intercession for them" (Heb. 4:16; 7:25; see also Rom. 8:31-35).

Jesus' Real Temptation and the "Godforsakenness" of the Cross

Christians do not serve an impotent Lord, but one who represents their cases before the God of the universe (who so loved us that He "gave" Christ for this work [John 3:16]) as victor and conqueror of Satan at the cross. According to the book of Revelation, "the accuser of our brethren has been thrown down, who accuses them day and night before our God." Christians are conquerors with Christ, their intercessor, through "the blood of the Lamb" (Rev. 12:10, 11). Even though Satan roundly lost the war at the cross and Resurrection, he perseveres in sheer audacity to accuse both repentant sinners and God, thereby continuing to demonstrate his principles and character.

A second aspect of Christ's heavenly work is that of judgment. While the cross judged sin once and for all, it still remained to be seen who would accept His substitutionary work. Those who do have "eternal life," but those who reject the Son are still under "the wrath of God" (John 3:36). Thus Jesus repeatedly taught that human beings would receive two kinds of rewards, depending on how they chose to relate to Him and to the principles of His kingdom. Some will acquire immortality when He comes again in the clouds, while others will face eternal damnation (Matt. 25:31-46; 1 Cor. 15:51-54; John 5:28, 29).

The New Testament teaches that God's judgment concerning each individual's eternal reward will have finished before the Second Coming (Matt. 16:27). When concluded, every living person will have made his or her decision for or against Christ, and then the decree of Revelation 22:11 will go forth from God's heavenly sanctuary: "Let the evildoer still do evil, and the filthy still be filthy, and the righteous still do right, and the holy still be holy." The Second Coming will take place soon after that final decree, and Christ will appear in the clouds of heaven bringing all their just rewards (Rev. 22:12; Matt. 16:27).

Thus, just as the Levitical service had a day of atonement (Yom Kippur), so there was to be a time of judgment in the heavenly ministry of Christ (Lev. 16; Rev. 14:6, 7; Dan. 7:10, 22, 26). It is of utmost importance to note that God's judgment does not seek to keep people out of heaven, but rather get them in. The God who gave Jesus for our sins is for us rather than against us. Judgment is "for the saints," and God will "vindicate" His people (Dan. 7:22; Deut. 32:36). Although the Levitical day of atonement was a period of heart searching and judgment, it ended with a time of rejoicing.[53] In like manner, God's people will rejoice with the results of Christ's ministry of judgment. It is Satan who has "led men to conceive of God as a being whose chief attribute is stern justice" and as one who is against us.[54] That is all part of his original lie that God cannot be trusted.

The great truth of the gospel is that God is for us. Not only did He give Christ to be our propitiation on the cross, but He has "committed all judgment unto the Son. . . . He that heareth my word, and believeth on him that sent me," Jesus promised, "hath everlasting life, and shall not come into condemnation" (John 5:22-24, KJV; compare Rom. 8:l).[55]

At the completion of His work in heaven, Christ will return to earth, bringing all their just "recompense" (Rev. 22:12; Matt. 16:27). Those who have accepted what He has done for them and in them will receive eternal life, while those who have rejected it will reap the wrath of God (John 3:36; Rev. 6:16, 17). We read in the book of Hebrews that "Christ, having been offered once to bear the sins of many, will appear a second time, not to deal with sin [that was the purpose of His life, death, resurrection, and heavenly ministry] but to save those who are eagerly waiting for him" (Heb. 9:28).

But even at the second coming of Christ the plan of salvation is not complete. The great final stage in Satan's defeat will take place during the centuries after the Second Advent.

---

[1] Taylor, *Atonement in New Testament Teaching,* p. 214; Taylor, *Jesus and His Sacrifice,* p. 304. Cf. Macquarrie, *Principles of Christian Theology,* p. 311.

[2] "Philippians," in *The Seventh-day Adventist Bible Commentary* (Washington, D.C.: Review and Herald, 1953-1957), vol. 7, p. 154. Cf. G. Braumann, "*Morpheē,*" in *The New International Dictionary of New Testament Theology,* ed. Cohn Brown, vol. 1, p. 706.

[3] S. E. Johnson, "*Kenosis,*" in *The Interpreter's Dictionary of the Bible,* ed. G. A. Buttrick, vol. 2, p. 7. Cf. Edward Heppenstall, *The Man Who Is God* (Washington, D.C.: Review and Herald, 1977), pp. 67-80.

[4] Ellen G. White, *Youth's Instructor,* Apr. 25, 1901, p. 130.

[5] Vincent Taylor, *The Person of Christ in New Testament Teaching* (London: Macmillan; New York: St. Martin's Press, 1966), p. 77.

[6] W. M. Clow, *The Cross in Christian Experience* (Garden City, N.Y.: Doubleday, Doran & Co., 1928), p. 119; Forsyth, *Work of Christ,* p. 153; Ellen G. White, *Review and Herald,* Apr. 1, 1875.

[7] See White, *The Desire of Ages,* p. 24.

[8] Murray, *Redemption Accomplished and Applied,* p. 19.

[9] Stott, *Cross of Christ,* p. 235; White, *Steps to Christ,* p. 28.

[10] Michael Green, *I Believe in Satan's Downfall* (Grand Rapids: Eerdmans, 1981), p. 195.

[11] See Ellen G. White, *Review and Herald,* Apr. 1, 1875.

[12] John H. Yoder, *The Politics of Jesus* (Grand Rapids: Eerdmans, 1972), p. 33.

[13] Weatherhead, *A Plain Man Looks at the Cross,* p. 22.

[14] Dederen, "Atoning Aspects in Christ's Death," p. 307.

[15] See Raymond E. Brown, *The Gospel According to John,* Anchor Bible (Garden City,

Jesus' Real Temptation and the "Godforsakenness" of the Cross

N.Y.: Doubleday, 1966), vol. 1, p. 249.

[16] James Denney, *Jesus and the Gospel* (London: Hodder and Stoughton, 1908), p. 210.

[17] William Barclay, *The Gospel of Matthew*, Daily Study Bible (Edinburgh: The Saint Andrew Press, 1956, 1957), vol. 2, p. 162.

[18] Green, *I Believe in Satan's Downfall*, p. 206; Stott, *Cross of Christ*, p. 26.

[19] Oscar Cullmann, "Immortality of the Soul or Resurrection of the Dead?" in *Immortality and Resurrection*, ed. Krister Stendahl (New York: Macmillan, 1965), pp. 13, 14.

[20] "The Martyrdom of Polycarp," chap. 12, in *The Apostolic Fathers*, 2nd ed., trans. J. B. Lightfoot and J. R. Harmer, ed. and rev. by Michael W. Holmes (Grand Rapids: Baker, 1989), p. 139.

[21] Stott, *Cross of Christ*, p. 76.

[22] White, *The Desire of Ages*, p. 686.

[23] D. M. Baillie, *God Was in Christ* (New York: Charles Scribner's Sons, 1948), p. 182.

[24] E. Bethge, *Dietrich Bonhoeffer* (Collins, 1970), p. 830, quoted in Moltmann, *The Crucified God*, p. 146.

[25] See Macquarrie, *Principles of Christian Theology*, p. 322; Dale, *The Atonement*, p. xl.

[26] See, for example, chapters 3 and 4 of this book and such texts as John 1:29; Mark 10:45; Heb. 9:28; 1 Peter 2:24, 3:18; 2 Cor. 5:21; Gal. 3:13.

[27] Forsyth, *Cruciality of the Cross*, p. 37.

[28] See Denney, *Christian Doctrine of Reconciliation*, pp. 273, 274.

[29] Forsyth, *Work of Christ*, p. 135.

[30] White, *The Desire of Ages*, p. 753.

[31] Augustine *On the Trinity* 4. 3. 6.

[32] Moltmann, *The Crucified God*, p. 152.

[33] White, *Steps to Christ*, p. 13; Forsyth, *Cruciality of the Cross*, p. 26. Cf. White, *The Desire of Ages*, p. 753; Dale, *The Atonement*, p. lx.

[34] James Stalker, *The Trial and Death of Jesus Christ* (New York: Richard R. Smith, 1930), p. 254.

[35] William Barclay, *The Gospel of John*, Daily Study Bible (Edinburgh: Saint Andrew Press, 1955), vol. 2, p. 301.

[36] Ellen G. White, *Review and Herald*, Sept. 24, 1901, p. 615; R.C.H. Lenski, *The Interpretation of St. Matthew's Gospel* (Minneapolis: Augsburg, 1943), p. 1127.

[37] R. J. Campbell, *The New Theology* (New York: Macmillan, 1907), p. 124.

[38] White, *The Desire of Ages*, p. 758, 761, 764; White, MS 50, 1900. Cf. White, *Patriarchs and Prophets*, p. 70.

[39] Macquarrie, *Principles of Christian Theology*, p. 321.

[40] Colin E. Gunton, *The Actuality of Atonement* (Grand Rapids: Eerdmans, 1989), p. 81; Gustaf Aulén, *The Faith of the Christian Church*, trans. Eric H. Wahlstrom, 2nd ed. (Philadelphia: Muhlenberg, 1960), pp. 182, 184.

[41] White, *The Desire of Ages*, p. 761.

[42] George Eldon Ladd, *I Believe in the Resurrection of Jesus* (Grand Rapids: Eerdmans, 1975), p. 144.

[43] See Merrill C. Tenney, *The Reality of the Resurrection* (New York: Harper and Row, 1963), pp. 135-137.

[44] Stalker, *The Atonement*, p. 19.

[45] D. Bonhoeffer, quoted in McGrath, *Mystery of the Cross*, p. 159.

[46] Walker, *Gospel of Reconciliation*, p. 125; Green, *I Believe in Satan's Downfall*, p. 212.

[47] It is not the purpose of this book to present a detailed study of Christ's heavenly ministry. That is the part of the atonement that has received the most adequate Seventh-day Adventist treatment, even though interpretations vary widely. See, for example, such works

The Cross of Christ

as M. L. Andreasen, *The Sanctuary Service*, 2nd ed. rev. (Washington, D.C.: Review and Herald, 1947); Heppenstall, *Our High Priest*; Wallenkampf and Lesher, eds., *The Sanctuary and Atonement*. For works covering the historical development of the topic, see Roy Adams, *The Sanctuary Doctrine: Three Approaches in the Seventh-day Adventist Church* (Berrien Springs, Mich.: Andrews University Press, 1981); Paul A. Gordon, *The Sanctuary, 1844, and the Pioneers* (Washington, D.C.: Review and Herald, 1983); Frank B. Holbrook, ed., *Doctrine of the Sanctuary: A Historical Survey* (Silver Spring, Md.: Biblical Research Institute, General Conference of Seventh-day Adventists, 1989).

[48] George Eldon Ladd, "Historic Premillennialism," in *The Meaning of the Millennium: Four Views*, ed. Robert G. Clouse (Downers Grove, Ill.: InterVarsity, 1977), pp. 31, 29, 30. Cf. Forsyth, *Work of Christ*, p. 170.

[49] Denney, *Studies in Theology*, pp. 154, 170; Robinson, *Redemption and Revelation*, p. 270.

[50] Ellen G. White, *The Great Controversy Between Christ and Satan* (Mountain View, Calif.: Pacific Press, 1911), p. 489.

[51] See Heppenstall, *Our High Priest*, pp. 17-19.

[52] F. F. Bruce, *The Epistles of John* (Grand Rapids: Eerdmans, 1970), pp. 49, 50.

[53] See *Mishnah* tractates Yoma 7:4 and Taanith 4:8, quoted in Morris, *The Atonement*, pp. 79, 80.

[54] White, *Steps to Christ*, p. 11.

[55] That the RSV translation of "judgment" in John 5:24 actually means "condemnation" is evident from a comparison of verses 28 and 29, in which the same word is contrasted with the resurrection of life. The Bible is clear on a pre-Advent judgment that determines whether individuals personally have accepted Christ's sacrifice for sin. See, for instance, Matt. 22:1-14.

Chapter 6

The Universe's Problem With God and the Reason for the Millennium

Christ's work, we saw in chapter 5, was finished on the cross, but it is obviously not yet fully implemented. People continue to die and abuse one another. Christians still struggle with temptation and sin. If God defeated Satan 2,000 years ago, we might ask, why is the war still going on? The answer to that question is the topic of this chapter. God, as we shall see, has His reasons.

Our present situation is somewhat similar to that of Hitler's forces in early 1945. After the Normandy landings in June 1944, the failure of the desperate Battle of the Bulge in late 1944, the incessant bombings of German transportation and manufacturing systems, and the massive Russian offensive in the east, it was evident that the Allied nations would win the war. Yet Hitler would not surrender. He would not accept defeat until all was lost and destroyed.

Satan is like that. The demonstration aspect of the great struggle between good and evil still goes on. Satan continues to exhibit who he is, while God keeps on quietly but actively loving His bleeding world. Bible prophecy indicates that Satan's principles, already powerful in the social realm, will become more and more prominent as the end of the age approaches. The book of Revelation makes it evident that the issues in the conflict will become so clear that all individuals will be able to choose whether to align themselves on the side of God's principles and receive His "seal," or to opt consciously for the ideals of Satan's kingdom and thereby receive the "mark of the beast" (Rev. 13:11-14:12).

The revelator pictures "four angels" holding back the "winds" of strife and destruction while God seals His end-time servants (Rev. 7:1, 3, 4; see

The Cross of Christ

also Rev. 14:1-5). In the meantime, the pressures leading to ecological, social, and political explosion and disintegration continue to increase as Satan preempts large sectors of modern technology for his own destructive ends. From what the book of Revelation tells us, the final movements in the warfare between God and Satan will be both violent and worldwide. Satan has an agenda diametrically opposed to God's, but the Lord has promised to intervene in human history through Christ at the Second Advent. The great theme of the book of Revelation is that of divine victory as events advance toward an intolerable state.

The Climax of History, the World's Longest Battle, and God's Judgment on Sin

The great climax of history arrives in Revelation 19, with Christ symbolically pictured as galloping out of heaven on a white horse to engage Satan in the battle that eventually brings about the end of the struggle between good and evil (verse 11). We should see that picture of the Second Advent as a continuation of God's atoning, reconciling, saving work. "In his cross and resurrection," George Eldon Ladd writes, "Christ won a great victory over the powers of evil; by his second coming, he will *execute* that victory."[1]

One thing that takes place at the Second Advent is the resurrection of those who have died believing in Jesus (those who have accepted God's grace). While the wicked (those who have rejected God's grace) perish at Christ's advent (Rev. 19:19-21), the living and resurrected righteous rise up to meet Jesus in the air and He takes them to heaven (1 Thess. 4:15-17; 1 Cor. 15:51-53; John 14:1-3). Thus the earth is left without living people during the 1,000-year period of Revelation 20.

Christ, however, speaks of recompense not only for the righteous, but also for the wicked (Matt. 16:27). He also talks of two resurrections. "The hour is coming," He claims, "when all who are in the tombs will hear his voice and come forth, those who have done good, to the resurrection of life, and those who have done evil, to the resurrection of judgment ['damnation,' KJV]" (John 5:28, 29).

The rewards for both groups, of course, result from the decision of the pre-Advent judgment (Dan. 7:22-27). Jesus goes on to claim that His judgment is "just [fair or righteous]" because He is in harmony with the Father (John 5:30). Thus Jesus ties divine justice or righteousness to the decision as to who will come forth in the two resurrections. Such an assertion of righteousness in judgment, however, is far from being demonstrable proof

The Universe's Problem With God and the Reason for the Millennium

of the fact of justice—an especially important problem in a universe where Satan has insinuated that God could not in justice save some sinners without saving all of them.

What Jesus does not make clear in John 5 is that 1,000 years will separate the two resurrections, a point John later reveals in Revelation 20. According to that chapter, some people will be resurrected at the beginning of the 1,000 years (verse 4), while the "rest of the dead did not come to life until the thousand years were ended" (verse 5). The context indicates that the first resurrection of Revelation 20 is that of the righteous mentioned in John 5, while the second is that of "damnation" also mentioned in the Gospel. "Blessed and holy," writes the revelator, "is he who shares in the first resurrection" (verse 6). Those who come up in the second soon meet the consuming fire of the "second death" (verses 7-9).

Whereas the resurrection of the dead is a fairly common theme in Scripture, Revelation 20 is the only explicit mention of the 1,000-year period in the Bible. Theologians refer to the time period as the millennium (a Latin phrase meaning 1,000 years).

Christian interpretations vary widely concerning the significance of the millennium and its place in the flow of history. Ladd writes that "the New Testament nowhere expounds the theology of the millennium, that is, its purpose in God's redemptive plan." Yet, he claims, "in some way not disclosed in Scripture, the millennium is part of Christ's Messianic rule by which he puts all his enemies under his feet (1 Cor. 15:25)."[2]

The key to the millennium's purpose appears in Revelation 20:4, in which we find the concept of "judgment" once again. We will return to that point shortly.

Meanwhile, it is important to examine the context of Revelation 20. The immediate and obvious framework is the material in chapters 19 and 21. Robert Mounce points out that the recurring phrase "and I saw" of Revelation 19:11, 17, 19; 20:1, 4, 12; and 21:1 "appears to establish a sequence of visions which carries through from the appearance of the Rider on the white horse (Rev. 19:11) to the establishment of the new heaven and new earth (Rev. 21:1ff)." Ladd also sees a connected series of visions, with Revelation 18 telling of the destruction of Babylon, chapter 19 the destruction of the beast and false prophet, and chapter 20 the destruction of Satan himself.[3]

The last half of chapter 19, as mentioned above, pictures Christ's second advent. This time, however, He comes not as the sacrificial Lamb of God, but as the "King of kings and Lord of lords" who will make war on

The Cross of Christ

all evil (verses 11-21).

Then follows Revelation 20, after which we find a picture of Eden restored. John opens chapter 21 with a glimpse of "a new heaven and a new earth; for the first heaven and the first earth [that is, those polluted by sin and its results] had passed away." Next John sees the "holy city," God's "New Jerusalem," coming out of heaven with blessings from the throne room/sanctuary. God Himself will now dwell with His people and provide them with the full blessings of His covenant. "He will wipe away every tear from their eyes, and death [the penalty of sin] shall be no more, neither shall there be mourning nor crying nor pain any more, for the former things have passed away" (verses 1-4).

Revelation 20, then, pictures the events that take place between the Second Advent and the establishment of God's perfect kingdom on earth. The millennium spans the gap from the time when sin was still alive to the time when it is no more. The chapter is the crucial link between those two very different earthly contexts. It holds an important place in God's great plan of at-one-ment, or reconciliation. At the end of the 1,000-year period He finally eradicates the sin problem.

A further contextual understanding of Revelation 20 emerges from Revelation 16. Verses 12-16 describe the pouring out of the sixth plague. The passage identifies the three great symbolic adversaries of God—the dragon (identified as Satan in Revelation 12:9), the beast, and the false prophet. The three of them dispatch "demonic," wonder-producing spirits, "who go abroad to the kings of the whole world, to assemble them for battle on the great day of God the Almighty. . . . And they assembled them at the place which is called in Hebrew Armageddon." Verses 14 and 15 make it clear that God's "great day" for the battle is at the second coming of Christ.

That thought brings us back to Revelation's description of the Second Advent in chapter 19. Near the end of the chapter we find an account of the first part of the battle of Armageddon. "And I saw," John declares, "the beast and the kings of the earth with their armies gathered to make war against him who sits upon the horse and against his army" (verse 19). In the next verse we encounter two of our three acquaintances from chapter 16—the beast and the false prophet. Christ captures and then destroys them in "the lake of fire" (verse 20).

With those two enemies (representing the leadership of Satan's human agents on earth) out of the way, God turns to deal with the root of the problem—the devil himself. Chapter 20 opens with Satan being bound (in the sense that with the righteous in heaven and the wicked in their graves he has no one to tempt or deceive—see verses 3, 7, 8) for the 1,000-year period (verses 1-3). At the end of that time, Satan (the third and final adversary of God from Rev. 16:13) and all his works and the results of sin perish in "the lake of fire" (verses 10, 13-15). Armageddon, the final and decisive battle between Christ and Satan, is then over.

Thus Revelation 19 and 20 represent Armageddon as having two significant engagements—one at the beginning of the millennium and the other at the end.[4] The second Armageddon engagement finds God executing His ultimate wrath not only on Satan, but on those sinners who have refused to accept (1) His principles into their lives and (2) Christ's vicarious sacrificial propitiation (the basis of grace) that turned aside the divine wrath (judgment on sin). Those individuals and forces destroyed in Armageddon will be the ones that have chosen to remain in rebellion against God, His government, and His law of love. Following the final destruction of Satan and the sin problem, we witness in Revelation 21 and 22 the renovation of the earth into Eden restored (cf. 2 Peter 3:12, 13).

The Millennium and the Judgment "on" God

G. B. Caird claims that Revelation 20 has been "the paradise of cranks and fanatics . . . and literalists." Furthermore, "it bristles with questions." Why, he asks, must Satan be let loose to wreak further havoc after being firmly bound? And what claim does the devil have on God, that He is obliged to give him his due? Why the millennium? And what blessing do the righteous receive that makes it worth their while to wait 1,000 years for the greater bliss of the new earth?

Because the controversial chapter raises such troubling questions, Caird sees plenty of good reasons for leaving it out of the Bible. In the face of the disturbing and troublesome issues suggested by Revelation 20, he forcefully concludes that "the only safe inference is that *John included the millennium because it was an indispensable element in his vision of the future.*"[5]

The key to that "indispensable element" appears to lie in Revelation 20:4, where the text refers to those to whom "judgment was committed." Two questions arise from that short phrase: (1) Who will be passing judgment? and (2) What is the nature of the millennial judgment?

On the first question, Mounce suggests that "all we know for sure" from Revelation 20 "about the occupants of the thrones is that judgment is given to them." He then goes on to note other Bible passages that help identify those sitting on them. Jesus, for example, promised the disciples that they would sit on 12 thrones judging the 12 tribes of Israel (Matt. 19:28), and Paul told the Corinthian believers that "the saints will judge the world." They would even "judge angels" (1 Cor. 6:2, 3).[6] Furthermore, earlier in the book of Revelation we find Christ announcing that all who conquered would sit with Him on His throne (Rev. 3:21; 2:26). On the basis of these texts and others, Ladd indicates that the judges in Revelation 20:4 probably include all the saved, since "this would accord with the biblical theology as a whole, which gives to the saints a share in the eschatological rule of Christ."[7]

But what is the function of their judgment? What remains to be judged? After all, the saints have already been determined worthy to come up in the first resurrection (Luke 20:35), and the wicked have obviously been found to be unworthy, since they do not rise until the second resurrection. *The judgment of Revelation 20 is obviously not to see who is saved or lost.* The decision regarding the fate of all human beings will have taken place before the Second Coming. At Christ's return all will have received their just rewards.

But were the rewards actually just? Did God really do the right thing in saving the saints while condemning those awaiting the second resurrection?

Such questions bring us back to the troubling Bible passages with which we opened this book. Never forget the total shock of both the sheep and the goats in the judgment scene of Matthew 25. "Why me?" ask some of those judged as unrighteous. They may have kept the law as perfectly as they could, yet they are lost. Why? Because, claims Jesus, they did not really love their neighbors. They didn't really care about the sick, the poor, and the downtrodden. Thus they had not internalized the principles of God's kingdom. Merely keepers of the letter of the law, they were out of harmony with its spirit of love.

Those judged to be sheep, having internalized the spirit of the law, but not being necessarily as dedicated as the Pharisees to a total life of consciously observing the outward aspects of the law, are equally surprised. Neither group receives what they think they deserve (Matt. 25:31-46).

If both sides in this parable show such surprise at the nature of their final rewards, how do we know that God handed them out correctly?

That brings me to the perplexing text of Matthew 7:21-23. There Jesus declares that "not every one who says to me, 'Lord, Lord,' shall enter the kingdom of heaven. . . . On that day many will say to me, 'Lord, Lord, did we not prophesy in your name, and cast out demons in your name, and do many mighty works in your name?' And then will I declare to them, 'I never knew you; depart from me, you evildoers.'"

Such sayings seem to be rather arbitrary. Obviously such people were Christian believers of some sort. Not only that, they appear to have possessed some powerful spiritual gifts. How can God be so sure He is rejecting the right individuals?

The entire problem, as we noted in chapter 1, is complicated by God's grace. *Remember that God in His grace gives people what they do not deserve.* Thus we saw my essential agreement with the older son in the parable of the prodigal in Luke 15, when I first read it as a 19-year-old agnostic. And thus also my grumbling along with the laborers who had toiled through the heat of the day only to get paid the same amount as those who had worked only the last hour (Matt. 20:1-16). Giving people what they don't deserve did not sit well with my human sense of justice. The problem even gets worse when one takes into account the fact that the rewards are eternal—immortal life versus eternal damnation (see Rom. 6:23).

And what if God gets so wild with grace that He gives it to some guy like Hitler or Stalin or people you personally know to have sexually abused 2-year-old children?

Can God really be trusted? That is the most important question of the universe. After all, look at the mess He allows to go on year after year. He has permitted thousands of years of murder, rape, and sins of every sort. "If God were good," C. S. Lewis writes in summarizing the skeptic's position, "He would wish to make His creatures perfectly happy, and if God were almighty, He would be able to do what He wished. But the creatures are not happy. Therefore, God lacks either goodness, or power, or both."[8] How can we have any confidence in such a Being?

And, as we also saw in chapter 1, one person dying for another doesn't seem to be much of a solution. Satan from the time of Cain has challenged the validity of substitutionary sacrifice, claiming that God is arbitrary and that there is no justice in having the best of human beings die so that a pack of criminals and rebels can get what they don't deserve. Neither grace nor forgiveness seems to be completely moral. How can God justify (declare as righteous) some people and destroy others eternally when all have sinned? And what is He going to do with those who were early turned from God by their parents or who were born into non-Christian cultures in which they had never heard the name of Jesus?

In short, the most important questions ever asked are "Can God be trusted?" and "If He can be, on what basis?"

The Cross of Christ

That is what the millennium is all about. Its purpose is to provide the saints with the time and opportunity to pass judgment (Rev. 20:4) on God's judgment on sin and His solution in Christ. By extension, because of His judicious openness (see below on Dan. 7:10), the millennial judgment is the final phase of judgment by a concerned universe on how God has handled the sin problem on this earth, the lesson book of the entire cosmos (1 Cor. 4:9).

The millennial judgment is the universe's juridic validation of God's justice and righteousness in justifying and eternally saving those who have accepted Christ's sacrifice, while forever destroying other individuals who also sinned. Can God do this and still be trustworthy and just? That, as we saw in chapter 4, was the underlying problem Paul wrestled with in Romans 3:21-26 (cf. 1 John 1:9-2:2). Earlier in Romans 3, the apostle had been concerned that God might be "justified" in His words, and "prevail" when He was "judged." Here Paul quoted the Septuagint version of Psalm 51, in which David dealt with the blamelessness of God in His judgment on and sentencing of sin (Rom. 3:4; Ps. 51:3, 4).

Thus, B. A. Gerrish writes, there is a sense in which "even God may be said to be justified."⁹ On a cosmic scale the great millennial judgment is the validation of God's judgment on sin so that everyone sees the justice of His solution and that it is both the best and the only answer to the sin problem.

It is crucial that all questions about God and His righteousness be settled before He destroys sinners and Satan in the second death at the end of the millennium (Rev. 20:9-15). After that point it will be too late. Thus the cruciality of the 1,000-year period that takes place between the two resurrections.

My guess is that life during the millennium will not be a completely peaceful time. Rather, it will be a period of healing and questioning and probably some weeping. How would you feel, for example, if you were to meet the murderer of your youngest child in the millennial kingdom? Especially how would you react if, as far as you could tell, that person had gone to execution kicking, cursing, and unrepentant? There will be some saved like that. We know of one who first found Jesus on the cross (Luke 23:39-43; Matt. 27:44).

Or how would you feel if you discovered that one of the most saintly Christians you had ever known had failed to arise at the first resurrection?

And what about family members you loved and felt you could never live without? Sons, daughters, wives, husbands, mothers, fathers, and others with whom we shared closeness may be among the missing.

What will your attitude be toward the God who intends to "execute" His judgment upon them at the end of the millennium? Could you really love and trust such a Being?

Coming to grips with those questions, feelings, and attitudes will be part of what the millennium must accomplish. As in the pre-Advent phase of the judgment, God desires to keep no secrets. In that earlier phase "ten thousand times ten thousand" angelic beings witnessed the proceedings (Dan. 7:10). The same kind of openness will be evident in the post-Advent phase of judgment.

Those resurrected will have a chance to examine and pass judgment on the evidence God has collected. The Bible speaks of books of judgment (Dan. 7:10; 12:1; Rev. 20:11, 12; Phil. 4:3). The presence of these books, H. B. Swete concludes, indicates that "the sentence of the Judge is not arbitrary; it rests upon written evidence."[10]

During the time the Bible was being written, of course, there were few, if any, books as we know them. People kept records in scrolls or on clay tablets. Since that time record-keeping has progressively advanced to bound books and then to computer technology.

Revelation 20:11, 12 mentions two kinds of books—the book of life and another type, seemingly standing in contrast to the book of life. They, Caird writes, "are the record books, containing all the evidence that the court needs if men are to be judged by their deeds." The book of life, Ladd suggests, "includes the names of all who have believed in Christ."[11]

Revelation 20:11, 12 mentions those books in connection with the very last act of judgment at the end of the millennium, when God pronounces final sentence. The "books" had earlier been used in the pre-Advent judgment of Daniel 7, and it is reasonable to suppose that the saints will also employ them during the millennial judgment. After all, the truth has nothing to lose from open investigation, and God's trustworthiness is the issue at hand. Just as He condescended to show the angels His justice and His righteousness in dealing with sinners in the pre-Advent judgment, so He does the same for the redeemed during the millennium.[12]

God's record-keeping system is undoubtedly much more advanced than human ones that use computer technology and sophisticated audiovisual devices. Since God is more concerned with motives than with outward behavior, it seems safe to assume that His record-keeping system includes human thoughts and motivations as well as the actions themselves.

With that in mind, let us go back to our questions about why some people obviously destined for hell come up in the resurrection of the righteous, while some of those we felt should have been in the first resurrection remain in their graves awaiting the second. "Why, God?" is the question that demands an answer. "How can You justify this or that particular decision?"

In answer, God points to the record "books." I respond by pushing the "computer button" representing the name of my favorite preacher—a person who I believed to be a saint of saints, but one who is still sleeping in the earth after the beginning of the millennium.

Suddenly, the record of his life flashes onto the screen in Technicolor and octophonic sound (or whatever type of information storage system God has). There for me to see is the fact that my preacher friend's inner life did not match up with his outer. In fact, to my surprise, I learn that even his outward life was different from what he claimed to believe, especially when he was "far enough" away from home or behind closed doors. The shocking realization hits me that he was not in harmony with God's principles and would not be happy in heaven.

With true heartache I turn off his record, realizing in a stab of shock that God had been right after all. Not being satisfied with that one case, however, I check out several more. Each time I reach the same conclusion—God is right. Knowing more about my closest friends than I did, He had done the best thing.

On the other hand, some of those who arose "with" the saints shock me just as much as those who did not. There obviously had been a frightful mix-up. I don't want to say much about it, but finally I just can't stand it any longer. So I go to the books of condemnation and push the button for a person "I know" to have been an unrepentant child abuser to the very end of his earthly life.

All I get is a blank at first, but then a signal flashes on the heavenly "computer screen," indicating that I am in the wrong document file. Rather haltingly approaching the "book of life" files, I again hit this person's "button." To my genuine surprise, I find his name and "experience" his conversion through God's sophisticated technology. The record shows that he has a new heart and mind and truly loves Jesus, even though, because of the last-minute (the eleventh hour of Matthew 20:6) nature of his conversion, he didn't have much earthly time to demonstrate his new attitudes and actions.

Stunned, and not completely sure, I shut off the machine. For a while I don't feel comfortable around this individual, even though he has come

The Universe's Problem With God and the Reason for the Millennium

up as a "saint." But from a distance I observe him from time to time, only to discover that God truly knew what He was doing. This "new man" is certainly a saint if I ever saw one. The full force of God's redeeming love and transforming power hits me as I realize the miracle that I have witnessed. "God," I almost shout, "is just and righteous and His judgments are true in every case." I have nothing but praise for Him.

But I have a friend who still isn't convinced that everything is right. She had loved her oldest son with fierce devotion throughout her long years of earthly motherhood. He had been what we had called a "good boy" during our time on earth. That is, he had been a good boy up until he was 23 years old. That was when his father had died.

During that year the young man turned against all he had once stood for. At first it was only a case of the outward signs of remorse in response to the great injustice that had befallen him. But then it turned into deep-seated rebellion. Feeling abused himself, he developed a character that consistently mistreated others.

His mother, as you might expect, was deeply upset by the physical loss of her husband and the spiritual loss of her son. Unlike the son, however, she did not turn against God. In fact, the experience softened her. After all, hadn't God lost His "beloved" on the cross? Her response to her husband's death was one of daily prayer for her rebellious son. Strong in faith that he would be in the kingdom, she went to her deathbed firmly believing that he would be converted. But, she hastened to add, if he were not, she did not want to be in heaven either. Never could she be happy without her boy.

I know her struggles and her convictions, because I was there when she died, and I later conducted her funeral. After her death I continued to work with the son, but to no avail. He was finally shot three times and killed while resisting federal agents in a drug crackdown.

I am glad to meet the mother soon after the first resurrection. As I expected, she has been looking in vain for her wayward treasure. She asks me what I know of him, and I fill her in on the newspaper stories. I then suggest that she go to the divine record system to get the full story. Feeling she needs support, I volunteer to sit through the experience with her. She views it again and again and again.

His case seems plain enough to me, but she is devastated, weeping profusely. Somewhere I had been taught that there would be no tears after the second coming of Christ, but I am beginning to realize that I must have been wrong. I check my Bible and find that it plainly promises that all tears

113

will be wiped away *after* the millennium (Rev. 21:4; compare Isa. 65:17-19), but that it gives no such assurances for the millennial period itself.

My weeping friend still isn't sure she wants to be in the kingdom if her son is not there. At that point I suggest that we "experience" the video of his life one more time. On this viewing I stop it from time to time, trying to help her realize that her son could not possibly be happy in God's kingdom, because everything he stood for diametrically opposed God's law of love.

I tell her the story of the first time I had dinner with a preacher. Back in those days, not knowing any clergy, I thought they were all perfect, or at least pretty close to it. But then, when I was 19 years old, I began to attend church so that I could spend more time with my girlfriend. Soon I concluded that I had made a mistake, because before I knew it we had been invited to dinner by the young preacher and his wife. The day of the dinner was the longest and one of the most miserable in my life up to that point. I had dreaded it all week, and it turned out to be more uncomfortable than I had expected. Being totally out of harmony with his principles, I had to watch everything I did, said, and how I said it.

Since that day I have often thought about what it would be like to spend eternity in the presence of the omniscient God if I were out of harmony with Him. Such an experience would be more like a living hell than heaven.

Using my personal experience, I try to help my friend understand what C. S. Lewis had enabled me to see back before the Second Advent. Lewis taught that there are only three possible states of existence: (1) to be God, (2) to be like God, or (3) to be miserable.[13] Lewis's third category represents the end result of lives out of harmony with God's character of giving and love. People in that group would be doubly miserable in the company of a holy Deity.

Ellen White teaches a similar perspective when she writes that "the sinner could not be happy in God's presence; he would shrink from the companionship of holy beings. Could he be permitted to enter heaven, it would have no joy for him. The spirit of unselfish love that reigns there—every heart responding to the heart of Infinite Love—would touch no answering chord in his soul. His thoughts, his interests, his motives, would be alien to those that actuate the sinless dwellers there. . . . *Heaven would be to him a place of torture*; he would long to be hidden from Him who is its light, and the center of its joy." The wicked, she continues, are not excluded from heaven by some arbitrary decree. Rather, "they are shut out by their own unfitness for its companionship."[14]

My friend, the distraught mother, is beginning to realize that God is doing what is best for her boy. It hurts deeply for her to recognize that fact, but more and more clearly she discovers that the God of love could not and would not force anyone to be saved.

She even starts to grasp the fact that eternal annihilation is better than eternal misery—the fruit of sin. Through her reddened eyes she begins to see a new aspect of God's love. She does not like all that she finds, but she realizes that God is making the very best out of a disastrous situation—that He still wants the very best for her son. At last, despite her tears, she acknowledges that her son could never be happy in heaven. Also she recognizes that the best and most loving alternative would be for him to be as if he had never been (we will return to this topic below). *My motherly friend finally sees that God's solution is not merely the best solution, but the only solution to the sin problem.*[15]

The Verdict "for" God and the Apocalyptic Doxologies

At this point we need to look at a prominent theme that runs throughout the book of Revelation. Often bursting forth in songs of praise, it proclaims the worthiness, justice, and truthfulness of God.

Revelation 4 and 5, for example, repeatedly declare God's worthiness in the context of the heavenly throne room/sanctuary. "*Worthy* art thou, our Lord and God, to receive glory and honor and power" (Rev. 4:11). In Revelation 5 John wept because he could find no one "worthy" to unseal the mysterious scroll (verse 4). Then the Lamb entered, and the heavenly beings "sang a new song, saying, '*Worthy* art thou to take the scroll and to open its seals, *for thou wast slain and by thy blood didst ransom men to God*'" (verse 9). Shortly the numberless host of heaven followed that song by "saying with a loud voice, '*Worthy is the Lamb who was slain*, to receive power and wealth and wisdom and might and honor and glory and blessing!'" (verse 12).

In these passages it is of more than passing interest to note that the "worthiness" of Christ to undo the seals of the scroll of salvation history is directly related to His propitiatory sacrifice on the cross. It was that sacrifice, Paul claims, that shows God's righteousness in justifying sinners through grace (Rom. 3:24-26; cf. 1 John 1:9-2:2).

The second major round of worshipful doxologies occurs during the pouring out of the seven last plagues—a period of divine judgment. At least three times chapters 15 and 16 praise God's justice and truthfulness.

The Cross of Christ

"*Just art thou in these thy judgments,*" the angel proclaims at the pouring out of the third bowl. The altar responds with the cry: "Yea, Lord God the Almighty, *true and just are thy judgments!*" (Rev. 16:5, 7; see also 15:3, 4).

The third series in Revelation's doxological sequence takes place at the Second Coming. Chapter 19 opens with "a great multitude in heaven, crying, 'Hallelujah! *Salvation and glory and power belong to our God, for his judgments are true and just*'" (verses 1, 2). Then, later in the chapter, the coming Christ on His white horse "is called *Faithful and True, and in righteousness he judges and makes war*" (verse 11).

Now either the heavenly hosts and/or the apostle John has an unhealthy fascination with the topic of God's truthfulness, justice, and worthiness to judge, or it is a central problem in the conflict between good and evil. The present book, of course, has taken the latter position. I have suggested that whereas the heavenly hosts were largely convinced of the justice of God at the cross, they will have had *all* their questions answered by the time of the second advent of Christ in Revelation 19. The resurrected saints will have the same opportunity to validate God's righteousness in solving the sin problem during the millennial judgment of Revelation 20. The purpose of that judgment is to clear up any final questions before God puts an end to sin. Thus He provides both adequate time and adequate records, that He might stand vindicated before all created beings.

At the end of the millennium, after the universe has settled all questions concerning God's righteousness and trustworthiness, God raises the wicked. At that time, the Bible says, Satan is loosed from his prison and goes "out to deceive" those who come up in the second resurrection. He gathers his multitude together for the second half of Armageddon, and they surround "the camp of the saints." At that point, fire flashes down from heaven and *consumes* them (Rev. 20:7-9).

For years I wondered why God would raise the wicked merely to snuff them out again. Robert Mounce writes that "perhaps the most reasonable explanation for this rather unusual parole is to make plain that neither the designs of Satan nor the waywardness of the human heart will be altered by the mere passing of time." Ellen White is even more specific. "In his last great effort to dethrone Christ, destroy His people, and take possession of the city of God, the archdeceiver" is "*fully unmasked.*"[16] In their last destructive moves, Satan and his followers provide one final validation on the correctness of God's judgment. They have not changed, having come out of the grave with the same character they had upon entering it.

With all the universe satisfied that Satan's principles lead to animosity, destruction, and death, God is at last free to deal decisively with the sin problem without creating fear and without spreading the doubt that Satan had insinuated concerning His love. It is from that perspective that Revelation 20:11-15 presents the last great act of divine executive judgment. At that point in history, God eradicates Satan, his followers, and the results of sin. Being thrown into the "lake of fire," they are "consumed" (verses 15, 9).

Strange as it may sound at first, God demonstrates His mercy even in the final destruction of the wicked. God wants the best for all His creatures. He wants their happiness. By the time of the Second Advent, He will have done everything He can to reach down and rescue people from their alienation and selfishness, but some will have rejected His outreach. The Lord will not force His love on those who spurn His grace. The acceptance of the principles of love and the healing they bring cannot be coerced. Satan's experiment with sin will have fully demonstrated that the way of sin and selfishness ultimately leads to self-destructive misery. Caught in a paradox, God can either let sinners continue to exist in endless unhappiness, or He can mercifully put them out of their self-chosen misery. With no other choices, God opts for the latter.

His choice, however, has been misunderstood and perverted beyond recognition. One of the most misleading theories in religious history is the one claiming that the merciful and loving God of the Bible will torture people unmercifully forever and ever in endless flames. That theory certainly casts doubt on God's character by making Him into kind of an infinite Hitler.[17] Perpetuating the original accusation of God through the ages, it proclaims that God truly is unjust and cannot be trusted. Beyond that, it furthers the unnatural fear of Him that entered with sin in Genesis 3. In fact, it is a continuation of Satan's first lie to Eve—"You will not die" (Gen. 3:4).

To the contrary, God said that the wages of sin is death, not immortality in hell (Rom. 6:23). Thus Revelation 20 makes it explicit that hell-fire "consumes" the wicked (verse 9). The results are eternal. They will be burned up and be as if they had never been (Mal. 4:1).

The imagery of the lake of fire, Michael Green suggests, "probably denotes final and irreversible ruin and *annihilation* rather than endless torment." Another Oxford scholar, John Wenham, comes to similar conclusions when he writes that "it might be nearer the mark to think of their end as a *merciful euthanasia* than as a callous execution."[18]

The bottom line on who will be in heaven, it seems, is determined by the standard of who will be happy there. All who could be happy with God will be there. Those with that attitude, of course, will be willing to live in harmony with God's great law of love (they will live lives of grace), which will affect every aspect of their existence. But those rejecting God's way are laid to permanent rest.

Thus God's approach is not endless torture for His erring children, but endless sleep in death. In that context, Emil Brunner's startling statement that "the wrath of God is the love of God" makes good sense. In His judgment on sin, the Lord does the best thing possible in a perplexing situation. Punishment, P. T. Forsyth writes, must be viewed "as an indirect and collateral necessity, like the surgical pains that make room for nature's curing power."[19] God's solution once again demonstrates that He is righteous and trustworthy.

Ellen White pens that by the end of the millennium "the whole universe will have become witnesses to the nature and results of sin. And its utter extermination, which in the beginning would have brought fear to angels and dishonor to God, will now vindicate His love and establish His honor before the universe of beings who delight to do His will." Because all the universe is satisfied that they can trust God and that Satan's principles lead to deterioration and death, she goes on to say that sin will never arise again. "A tested and proved creation will never again be turned from allegiance to Him whose character has been fully manifested before them as fathomless love and infinite wisdom." Satan's rebellion will be a lesson to the universe throughout eternity on the nature of sin. Thus the history of this terrible experiment will be a "perpetual safeguard" to God's universe.[20]

The Desire of Ages expresses similar thoughts: *"Through Christ's redeeming work the government of God stands justified.* The Omnipotent One is made known as the God of love. Satan's charges are refuted, and his character unveiled. Rebellion can never again arise. Sin can never again enter the universe. Through eternal ages all are secure from apostasy."[21]

Theoretically, of course, sin could emerge again. After all, it appeared unexplainably and spontaneously the first time because of the power of choice that God gave His creatures. God has not taken away that power, nor can He without changing His own nature. Thus it is theoretically possible for sin to rise a second time, but it is safe to say that it would not be able to rise very high. The entire universe will have come to love and trust God, and all will have seen the results of sin. God, therefore, will be in a position to put down any rebellion immediately. The great experiment with sin will never need to be repeated. The cross of Christ demonstrated once and for all the love of God and the malignity of sin.

Sin, we must never forget, is not a personal aberration. Rather, Brunner rightly claims, it is "an attack on God's honor." It is an assault on the cosmic moral order.[22] Because of what sin is, the greatest challenge God ever faced was to meet it responsibly and decisively in a manner that would preserve the moral order of the universe and at the same time demonstrate both His love and His justice.

The crisis of sin, as emphasized in chapter 1, is not merely a human crisis, but a divine one. Sin deeply affected the stability of God's universe. Well aware of the magnitude and subtlety of the problem, God has not treated it lightly. His answer to the sin problem is the life and death of Jesus Christ and the extension of grace to sinners. "At the heart of the Christian doctrine of atonement," James Stewart pens, "stands the fact that if our sin has serious consequences for ourselves, it has terrible consequences for God."[23]

God gave of Himself to meet the problem. The life of Christ demonstrated that the divine law of love could be kept, while His death demonstrated both God's love and justice and Satan's hate and unfairness. Christ's sacrifice prepared the way for God to freely forgive on a moral basis by taking into account the full penalty of the broken law.

It was at the cross, Forsyth indicates, that God justified "Himself and His holy law. . . . If He had not vindicated His holiness to the uttermost . . . it would not be a kind of holiness that men could trust." Because the Lord has first justified Himself in holiness, He can also justify human beings and still be righteous.[24]

The fruits of God's great plan of reconciliation or at-one-ment through Christ, as we have repeatedly noted, are not just for Himself and earthlings. The New Testament pictures the sin problem as having cosmic proportions. Thus Paul could write: "We are not contending against flesh and blood, but against the principalities, against the powers, against the world rulers of this present darkness, against the spiritual hosts of wickedness in the heavenly places" (Eph. 6:12). The apostle also indicates that the implications of the solution have universal import. Thus he asserts that God is reconciling to Himself all things, "whether on earth or in heaven," through Christ's cross (Col. 1:20). The end result of God's program for handling sin will be "that at the name of Jesus every knee should bow, in heaven and on earth and under the earth, and every tongue confess that Jesus Christ is Lord, to the glory of God the Father" (Phil. 2:10, 11).

The Cross of Christ

Thus both the problem of sin and God's solution to that calamity affect the entire universe. "Wherever Christian teaching narrows the idea of the Atonement to a prospect less dazzling than this," Vincent Taylor argues, "it is untrue to the New Testament."[25]

It Is Really Finished

At the end of the millennium God stands vindicated and justified before the universe. With sin destroyed, the Holy City descends out of heaven so that God can re-create our planet to be the eternal home of the redeemed. All tears have been wiped away, and there is no more death, suffering, or sorrow (Rev. 21:1-4; 2 Peter 3:12, 13).

The atonement (at-one-ment) is finally completed. All who can be reconciled to God have been. "The great controversy is ended," Ellen White writes. "Sin and sinners are no more. The entire universe is clean. One pulse of harmony and gladness beats through the vast creation. From Him who created all, flow life and light and gladness, throughout the realms of illimitable space. From the minutest atom to the greatest world, all things, animate and inanimate, in their unshadowed beauty and perfect joy, declare that God is love."[26]

John the revelator beheld "a great multitude which no man could number, from every nation, from all tribes and peoples and tongues, standing before the throne and before the Lamb, clothed in white robes, with palm branches in their hands, and crying out with a loud voice, '*Salvation belongs to our God* who sits upon the throne, and to the Lamb!' And all the angels stood round the throne and round the elders and the four living creatures, and they fell on their faces before the throne and worshiped God, saying, 'Amen! *Blessing and glory and wisdom and thanksgiving and honor and power and might be to our God for ever and ever! Amen*'" (Rev. 7:9-12). All are convinced that the God of grace can indeed be trusted.

---

[1] George Eldon Ladd, *A Commentary on the Revelation of John* (Grand Rapids: Eerdmans, 1972), pp. 252, 253. (Italics supplied.)

[2] Ladd, "Historic Premillennialism," in Clouse, p. 39.

[3] Mounce, *Book of Revelation*, p. 352; Ladd, *Revelation of John*, p. 261.

[4] Cf. Henry Barclay Swete, *The Apocalypse of St. John* (Grand Rapids: Eerdmans, n.d.), pp. 256, 268.

[5] G. B. Caird, *The Revelation of St. John the Divine*, Harper's New Testament Commentaries (Peabody, Mass.: Hendrickson, 1987), pp. 249-251. (Italics supplied.)

[6] Mounce, *Book of Revelation*, pp. 354, 355.

[7] Ladd, *Revelation of John*, p. 263.

The Universe's Problem With God and the Reason for the Millennium

[8] Lewis, *Problem of Pain*, p. 26. See also John Hick, *Evil and the God of Love*, rev. ed. (San Francisco: Harper and Row, 1978), p. 5.

[9] B. A. Gerrish, "Justification," in *The Westminster Dictionary of Christian Theology*, ed. A. Richardson and J. Bowden, p. 314.

[10] Swete, *Apocalypse of St. John*, p. 272.

[11] Caird, *Revelation of St. John*, p. 259; Ladd, *Revelation of John*, p. 273.

[12] See Heppenstall, *Our High Priest*, p. 209.

[13] Lewis, *Problem of Pain*, p. 54.

[14] White, *Steps to Christ*, pp. 17, 18. (Italics supplied.) Cf. White, *The Great Controversy*, p. 670.

[15] Perhaps I should point out the elements of fact and fiction in the above account of millennial investigation. The account, as I see it, is true to millennial purpose. It is obviously parabolic, but my dinner with the preacher did take place and I did have that reaction.

[16] Mounce, *Book of Revelation*, p. 361 (cf. p. 354); White, *The Great Controversy*, p. 670. (Italics supplied.)

[17] See George R. Knight, "The Infinite Hitler," *Signs of the Times*, July 1997, pp. 10-13.

[18] Green, *I Believe in Satan's Downfall*, p. 218; John W. Wenham, *The Enigma of Evil: Can We Believe in the Goodness of God?* (Grand Rapids: Zondervan, 1985), p. 38, n. 9. (Italics supplied.)

[19] Emil Brunner, *Man in Revolt*, trans. Olive Wyon (Philadelphia: Westminster, 1947), p. 187; Forsyth, *Work of Christ*, p. 135.

[20] White, *The Great Controversy*, pp. 504, 499.

[21] White, *The Desire of Ages*, p. 26. (Italics supplied.)

[22] Brunner, *The Mediator*, p. 444.

[23] James S. Stewart, *A Faith to Proclaim* (New York: Charles Scribner's Sons, 1953), p. 69.

[24] Forsyth, *Work of Christ*, p. 136.

[25] Taylor, *Atonement in New Testament Teaching*, p. 168.

[26] White, *The Great Controversy*, p. 678. A point of special interest is that the first three words of the first volume and the last three words of the last one of Ellen White's five volume set depicting the great controversy theme are the same: "God is love." To her, that was the point at issue in the struggle between Christ and Satan and it was what God demonstrated in His multiplex plan of atonement.

Chapter 7

Radical Faith's Response to the Cross

Some things are impossible to face with neutrality. The cross of Christ is one of them. A person either has to scoff at the "stupid naïveté" of a person who would die for those abusing Him, or one must stand in awe of such dedicated love.

The life of Christ makes distinct the boundary between two kingdoms, two ways of life. The one is built on self-giving, the other on self-getting. A person is either in harmony with Christ's values or upset by their strenuous demands.

Unfortunately, that boundary remains blurred even to most Christians, because churches tend to preach an emasculated Christ—a polite, moderate, well-behaved Christ. In such instances the church is not looking at the Christ of Scripture, but at a god created in the image of middle-class church members.

The Christ of the Bible preached a demanding message of radical discontinuity with the values of both the secular and the religious world around Him. The remarkable thing is that His message is just as much out of harmony with those churches that carry His name as it was with those religious leaders who crucified Him. For 2,000 years the Christian church has tried to explain away and soften the Sermon on the Mount, but it is still the world's most revolutionary manifesto. Jesus was out to change His world from the inside out.

Not only did Christ preach a violent message, but He died a violent death as the result of that message. His hearers found themselves forced to respond to the boldness of His actions and assertions. There is no middle ground with a man who claims to be God. C. S. Lewis put the issue bluntly when he wrote that Christ is either what He claims to be, or a lunatic, or the world's greatest deceiver and the "Devil of Hell."

Radical Faith's Response to the Cross

He is either God and Savior, or He is the archenemy of truthfulness.[1]

Christ's claims led to His crucifixion. He still presents us with an unavoidable choice. *Either we crucify Him, or we let Him crucify us. There is no middle ground with Jesus.*

Radical Faith

To come face to face with the cross of Christ is to encounter the astounding truth that the ultimate reality is not sin, alienation, death, or anything else we might glean from the daily news, "but a love which bears sin, taking . . . all its dreadful reality upon itself."[2] That is what the good news of the gospel is all about.

Martin Luther, the great sixteenth-century Reformer, never ceased to marvel at what Christ had done for him personally. To Luther, finding Christ was being "snatched . . . from the jaws of hell."[3] The Reformer's response to God's salvation was the same as Paul's—total dedication to the God who gave so much for him. The cross of Christ is a radical symbol of a radical reality, and it demands a radical response.

Modern expositors of the cross of Christ have consistently emphasized the "violent" nature of true faith. James Denney, for example, writes that "*faith* is not the acceptance of a legal arrangement; it *is the abandonment of the soul*, which has no hope but in the Saviour, *to the Saviour*. . . . *It includes the absolute renunciation of everything else, to lay hold on Christ*." Faith is a "*passion* in which the whole being of man is caught up and abandoned unconditionally to the love revealed in the Saviour." Such a response is "*the whole of Christianity*."[4]

More recently, Jürgen Moltmann has argued that "radical Christian faith can only mean committing oneself without reserve to the 'crucified God.'" Such commitment, he argues, is dangerous, because it offers no recipe for success. To the contrary, it thrusts people into confrontation with both their own selves and the world around them. "It does not bring man into a better harmony with himself and his environment, but into contradiction with himself and his environment."[5]

In a similar vein, P. T. Forsyth penned that Greek and philosophic wisdom uplifts the values of moderation, but not Christianity. "We cannot love God too much, nor believe too much in His love, nor reckon it too holy. *A due faith in Him is immoderate, absolute trust.*"[6]

Jesus set the stage for radical Christian response. He claimed that His mission was not to bring peace into the lives of His followers, but a sword. Radical faith would transform lives and infuse them with new principles—

principles at odds with those of "the ruler of this world." The resulting collision in value systems would set family members against one another and put converts to Christ in conflict with their world in general. Then Jesus went on to say that allegiance to Him comes before all other allegiances. "He who loves father or mother more than me is not worthy of me; and he who loves son or daughter more than me is not worthy of me; and he who does not take his cross and follow me is not worthy of me. He who finds his life will lose it, and he who loses his life for my sake will find it" (Matt. 10:34-39; see also Luke 14:25-33). On another occasion, Christ taught that "he who loves his life loses it, and he who hates his life in this world will keep it for eternal life" (John 12:25).

Such words are not those of a moderate. No wonder Christ was crucified. He stood flat against the value system of this world—and was hated for it. His violent teachings led to His violent death.

A reading of Acts and the Epistles gives one the impression that the disciples had become as immoderate as the Master. Something had happened in the lives of the apostles that transformed them. They were men obsessed with a mission. Its intensity impelled them to preach their gospel message throughout much of the known world of their time within a few decades.

The only kind of valid faith in Christ is the radical one of the cross, the faith of single-minded dedication. Anything less than that may be sufficient for "playing church," but it falls short of the total commitment that *is* Christianity.

The Death of a "Rebel" and the Birth of a "Saint"

"When Christ calls a man, he bids him come and die."[7] Dietrich Bonhoeffer's words reflect the one essential test of Christian discipleship. He has good authority for his statement. You will recall that Peter played the part of the tempter to Christ at Caesarea Philippi by telling Him that He did not need to die. After turning on Peter and addressing him as Satan, Jesus gave the disciples one of His most frightful teachings. "If any man would come after me, let him deny himself and take up his cross and follow me. For whoever would save his life will lose it, and whoever loses his life for my sake will find it" (Matt. 16:24, 25).

The mistake most people make when reading that passage is viewing it through 2,000 years of Christian history. The result is that they miss the stark meaning that it had for the disciples. To get at it, you have to put yourself in the place of those to whom Christ spoke. Jesus had just finished explicitly telling them that He was the Messiah. The very word "Messiah"

Radical Faith's Response to the Cross

filled their minds with visions of a kingdom of glory and power, one in which they, as His faithful assistants, would have key positions.

Then, while their hopes were at their highest, Jesus foretold His rejection and death. That was bad enough, but He also warned His followers that each of them would have his own cross.

Now, as we noted before, the idea of being crucified doesn't do much to our twenty-first-century imagination. We have never seen a crucifixion. The word has little personal meaning to us. But not for the disciples. When they saw a knot of Roman soldiers escorting a man through town carrying or dragging the beam of a cross, they knew it was a one-way trip. They regarded the cross as the cruelest and most humiliating of deaths—and one that the ruling Romans were more than willing to use at any opportunity to keep troublesome areas such as Palestine under control.

To Jesus and the disciples the cross symbolized death, and nothing else. The cross that Christ spoke of was not merely tolerating a nagging wife or a cantankerous husband.

We find the key to Jesus' meaning in the words "let him deny himself." Usually we think of self-denial in a limited sense, such as giving up something or doing without a luxury. For example, we interpret self-denial as abstaining from chocolate candy or some other special treat for a month so that we can contribute the money saved to a worthy cause, or we perceive it as foregoing the Sunday afternoon football game in order to spend time doing something with our family.

Now, such types of self-denial are undoubtedly included in what Jesus meant, but He was saying much more than that. "To deny oneself," writes William Barclay, "means in every moment of life to say no to self, and to say yes to God. To deny oneself means . . . to dethrone self and to enthrone God" as the center of our life. "To deny oneself means to obliterate self as the dominant principle of life, and to make God the ruling principle, more, the ruling passion of life."[8]

To understand Christ's intent, we need to remember what sin is all about. Sin, in its most basic meaning, is putting our "self" and our will rather than God and His will at the center of our life. It is rebellion against God in the sense that we choose to become ruler of our own lives. As a result, sin is saying no to God and yes to our self.

Thus when Christ talks of denying oneself, He means turning away from the idolatry of self-centeredness. He means conversion. Jesus, therefore, can associate self-denial with the cross. Luke helps us comprehend Christ's perspective when he notes that cross-bearing is to be a daily experience for His followers (Luke 9:23). Jesus was not speaking of a physical death, but of putting the self as the center of our lives on the cross as an instrument of death. He was calling for the total abandonment of selfishness every day, for constant surrender to the Father's will.

At this point we need to be careful. The Christian definition of self-denial is not self-hatred. It does not imply that we are worthless and should constantly be humming the tune for "a worm like me." The genuine and the counterfeit are often close neighbors. That is true with healthy and unhealthy versions of self-love. Jesus uplifted a healthy self-love. It lies, in fact, at the base of the golden rule and the second great commandment (Matt. 7:12; 22:39; Luke 6:31). I cannot love my neighbor unless I first love myself.

But healthy self-love is founded upon God's love for me rather than upon my intrinsic goodness. The fact that Jesus died for me on the cross indicates the extent of my "valuableness." But distorted self-love leaves God out of the center of the picture and places my lost self at its focal point. That self-centeredness then becomes the foundation of pride and selfishness. Jesus called for healthy self-love, but saw unwholesome versions of it as the source of the sin problem that originated with Lucifer.

To pass from the self-centered spirit of this world to the spirit of Christ, H. H. Farmer indicates, is not a matter of gentle growth or natural evolution. Rather, "it is an uprooting, rending, tearing, splitting and breaking, surgical-operation kind of thing, a . . . crucifixion."[9]

The center of the struggle is in the individual human will, "the governing power in the nature of man." Sin originates in self-centered willfulness. Thus Ellen White can write that "the warfare against self is the greatest battle that was ever fought. The yielding of self, surrendering all to the will of God, requires a struggle; but the soul must submit to God before it can be renewed in holiness." As Denney put it: "Though sin may have a natural birth it does not die a natural death; in every case it has to be morally sentenced and put to death."[10] That sentencing is an act of the will under the impulse of the Holy Spirit. Christ called it a crucifixion.

The daily crucifixion of the self is the constant surrendering of the human will to God's will, trusting that He knows what is best for us. It includes the recognition that we can do nothing to free ourselves from the meshes of the net of sin.

Christ had His cross, and we have ours. He died on His for our sins, in which He had no share; and we die on ours to all pride and self-reliance, that we might partake of His life. At the cross of Christ all our intellectual and moral independence finally shatters, and we freely admit our dependence on Him in every aspect of our lives.

From the point of view of the cross, the words of Christ take on new meaning: "Whoever would save his life will lose it," but "whoever loses his life for my sake . . . will save it" (Luke 9:24). The great discovery of Adam and Eve was that the way of self is the road to death.

At this juncture it is important to recognize that Christianity is not merely a way of dying, but also a way of living. Christianity is primarily a positive force, not a negative. The death of self as the center of existence sets the stage for Christian living.

Just as Christ's resurrection followed His death, so it is in the experience of each of His followers. "We were buried therefore with him by baptism into death, so that as Christ was raised from the dead by the glory of the Father, we too might walk in newness of life. For if we have been united with him in a death like his, we shall certainly be united with him in a resurrection like his." The Christian is "dead to sin and alive to God in Christ Jesus" (Rom. 6:4, 5, 11; cf. Col. 2:8-15).

God's ideal for His people is not a moral void, but a new life of fullness. That life begins with the death of the old one that was marked by egocentric selfishness. Repentance is an abhorrence of one's sin, accompanied by a responding to God's love in Christ. The Christian life is not merely the turning away from something, but the embracing of a new life.

Our initial crucifixion takes place when we finally surrender all human wisdom and effort to save self from the bondage of sin and we accept the work of Christ in our behalf. At that time, God justifies us and counts us as righteous. But that righteousness is not a mere legal fiction. At the same time that God justifies, He also begins the process of regeneration. Paul says that through His grace the Lord gives converted people new hearts and minds, new ways of looking at the world, and new motives for living in it (Col. 3:9, 10; Rom. 12:2; Eph. 4:22-24).

Ellen White writes that "God's forgiveness is not merely a judicial act by which He sets us free from condemnation. It is not only forgiveness *for* sin, but reclaiming *from* sin. It is the outflow of redeeming love that transforms the heart."[11]

In like manner, Raoul Dederen points out that "God's verdict that acquits us is also a creative act." Christ's substitutionary death is not "the entirety of the work of Christ." If it were, "then salvation would be an external transaction wrought outside of the believer" and would have "nothing to do with his ethical and spiritual life. But in the death of Christ the believer finds not only an objective atonement for sin but also deliverance from the power of sin."[12]

Paul, therefore, refers to the person who accepts Christ's work as a "new creation"—one for whom the old way "has passed away" and "the new has come" (2 Cor. 5:17). Christ saves us, Donald Bloesch writes, "not only by dying for us but also by being reborn within us by his Spirit."[13] Thus Paul could say: "I have been crucified with Christ; it is no longer I who live, but Christ who lives in me [through the presence of the Holy Spirit]; and the life I now live in the flesh I live by faith in the Son of God, who loved me and gave himself for me" (Gal. 2:20).

Christians, living in the power of Christ's resurrection, do not need to strive to win the victory over the devil. Christ did that. Their great need is to strive to stay surrendered to Christ so that they will continuously have God's power working in their lives (Phil. 2:12, 13). Because we face an enemy defeated at the cross, Forsyth writes that "we do not gain the victory; we are united with the Victor."[14]

The secret to the successful Christian life, of course, is staying surrendered. That brings us back to Paul's great statement that Christ "emptied himself" of His divine attributes at the incarnation, became a "servant," and "became obedient unto death, even death on a cross" (verses 6-8). We treated that text at some length in chapter 5, but what we did not emphasize there is that the apostle prefaced his remarks with "let this mind be in you, which was also in Christ Jesus" (verse 5, KJV).

Paul's admonition is for each believer to partake of Christ's humility. If Christ emptied Himself of all willfulness and self-serving, then it follows that we must also. As we saw in chapter 5, Christ relied on the power of the Spirit to perform His miracles and give Him the strength to follow the Father's will. Just as the great temptation in Christ's life was to become self-reliant and to do His own will, so it will be in ours.

Edward Heppenstall forcefully portrays the answer of Christ to that temptation of temptations. "Christ," he wrote, "was tempted to do what was contrary to God's will. But He willed to have no self-will; He made the will of God His own. He lived by faith in God alone. He ordered His life in accordance with the revelation given to Him."[15]

Living the surrendered life, of course, is nothing automatic. As Moltmann put it, the knowledge of Christ's cross brings a conflict of interest between the ideals of the "God who has become man and [the] man who wishes to become God."[16] Thus the meaningfulness of Paul's challenge: "Let this mind be in you, which was also in Christ Jesus."

As Jesus lived in complete dependence on His Father, so may we. That dependence, we should note, did not destroy Christ's personality, nor will it eradicate ours. Rather, it is a redirection of the activities and attitudes of each personality. It implies a reorientation of the entire life of the person converted to Christ.

The Cross and Daily Living

"I appeal to you therefore," Paul wrote to the church in Rome, ". . . to present your bodies as a living sacrifice, holy and acceptable to God. . . . Do not be conformed to this world but be transformed by the renewal of your mind" (Rom. 12:1, 2). "Living sacrifice" is a poignant phrase. A sacrifice is something totally dedicated to God. It is the "living" part of the phrase, however, that makes it a rich and difficult concept. Probably it is easier to die as a martyr for Christ in the excitement and tension of the moment than it is to live for Him for the duration of a lifetime.

The problem with living the Christian life, I have discovered, is that the temptation to "get off my cross" and do my own will rather than the Father's never ends. Constantly I find my temper rising when someone offends my precious self. Unlike Christ, I can't call down 12 legions of angels to defend me, but I am tempted to climb down from my cross and give my adversaries exactly what they deserve.

I like grace (getting what one does not deserve) when it is directed toward me, but it is not something I am tempted to be overly generous with when it comes to handing it out. It would be easier just to die once and for all and get it over with than to be a "living sacrifice." But, Paul is saying, God's standard is higher than that. Our entire existence is to be set aside for holy living, a life guided in its every aspect by God's principles.

Another interesting word in Romans 12:1, 2 is "transformed," which comes from a Greek word that we use in English as "metamorphosis." Metamorphosis is that mysterious process by which an awkward, sluglike caterpillar changes into an elegant and graceful butterfly. It denotes a transformation so radical that unless people knew better, they wouldn't even realize that it was the same life. That is what God wants to do in His children. Their lives are to be totally reshaped through the power of the Holy Spirit.

The new life of the Christian means a radically new relationship with God. Where once we were against Him, or neutral toward Him, the born-again experience is one of active dedication to God. Faith is a relationship with our Father. Beyond that, the faith relationship suggests a life orientation that structures all the Christian's daily activities and goals.

Thus the Christian not only dies for Christ, but lives for Him. One of the great paradoxes of the New Testament, Leon Morris suggests, is that salvation does not depend on anything we do, but on the other hand, we don't receive it without a response in godly living. Both Paul and Jesus taught that all people would ultimately be judged by their deeds and character (Matt. 7:21-27; Rom. 2:12, 13).[17]

The Bible says two important things about human deeds or works: (1) No one earns salvation by them (Gal. 2:16; Eph. 2:8, 9), and (2) No one is saved without them (James 2:17-20; Matt. 7:21-27). The two perspectives do not contradict each other. A new way of living, thinking, and acting is the natural fruit of a life rooted in Christ (John 15:5, 8, 10).

One of the great tragedies in the aftermath of the Reformation is that justification (God counting us righteous) became separated from sanctification (God making us righteous). In the desire to create distance between Reformation theology and that of Rome, the followers of the Reformers created an artificial dichotomy. Thus, Bonhoeffer reports, "Luther had said that grace alone can save; his followers took up his doctrine and repeated it word for word. But they left out its invariable corollary, the obligation of discipleship."[18]

In a similar line of thought, Denney asserts that "it has sometimes [been] forgotten that the great matter is not the distinction of justification and sanctification, but their connection, and that justification or reconciliation is a delusion unless the life of the reconciled and justified is inevitably and naturally a holy life." These two aspects of salvation are "the indivisible and all-inclusive response of the soul to Christ."[19] (*Sin and Salvation*, the sequel to *The Cross of Christ*, will treat this subject in greater depth).

The truly converted life is one that views all issues from the perspective of the cross. When we have the mind of Christ, we will see sin as Christ sees it, we will sorrow over its results as He sorrows over them, and we will be repelled by those things that repel Him.

For a Christian to continue to live in deliberate sin is a contradiction. "To account a man righteous who is a sinner and living in sin," Mildred Wynkoop argues, "would be to deny everything that cost Christ so much. God does not change His definition of *sin* to make it go away."[20]

James Stewart shares a similar insight when he writes that "to be united to Christ means to be *identified with Christ's attitude to sin*. . . . It means an assent of the whole man to the divine judgment proclaimed upon sin at the cross."[21] We are not really reconciled to God until we accept His way of life. The cross is not merely a theological riddle that God requires us to understand, pens Alister McGrath, but a "demand for faith and obedience." The converted sinner, we read in *Steps to Christ*, "will discern something of the depth and sacredness of God's holy law, the foundation of His government in heaven and on earth."[22]

The way of the cross is a way of life, one that will affect all our relationships just as radically as Adam and Eve's fall into sin in Genesis 3 did theirs. It will create a reorientation of our lives that will enable us through the power of the Holy Spirit to heal the manifold alienations we discussed in chapter 2.

The Christian life is one in which you will "love the Lord your God with all your heart" and "your neighbor as yourself" (Matt. 22:37, 39). Beyond that, the born-again life experiences a healing with its own self. Instead of blaming other people for our problems and attacking their sins (Gen. 3:11-13), Christians will "confess" their own sins and thus be forgiven and cleansed "from all unrighteousness" (1 John 1:9).

The life of the cross is one of service to others. Totally reversing human value structures, Jesus told His disciples, after James and John got caught red-handed lusting after the highest places in the coming kingdom, that "whoever would be great among you must be your servant, and whoever would be first among you must be slave of all. For the Son of man also came not to be served but to serve, and to give his life as a ransom for many" (Mark 10:43-45). We can sum up the entire Christian ethic as loving service to both God and humanity. Being reconciled to God means being reconciled to our neighbors (defined in the Gospels to include one's enemies [Luke 10:25-37; Matt. 5:43-48]).

The only problem with all these high ideals is putting them into practice. Friedrich Nietzsche said that "before we can believe in redemption, Christians must look more redeemed."[23] Talking about living a Christian way of life is one thing, but putting it into practice is quite another. Thus W. L. Walker can truthfully write that "it is the want of this Love in the practical everyday life that is the only real argument against Christianity."[24] On the other hand, Jesus said, "By this all men will know that you are my disciples, if you have love for one another" (John 13:35).

These thoughts bring us back to the so-called moral influence theory of the atonement, which we touched on several times in chapters 3 and 4. That view of Christ's work, as we noted, holds that Jesus died primarily to impress individuals with a sense of God's love, thereby softening their hearts into repentance and inspiring them to follow His example of "caringness" in their own lives. We earlier saw that while the moral influence position does have a great deal of truth in it, it is not a sufficient explanation of the cross.[25] Christ died not only to reveal God's love for us and to inspire us, but to bear our sins, pay the penalty for sin, and turn aside the divine judgment on sin from those who believe on Him.

It is the objective sacrifice of Christ on Calvary for sin that sets the stage for the subjective human response. R. C. Moberly was right when he wrote that in every individual the work of Christ must be "objective first, that it may become subjective. . . . It is first a historical fact, that it may come to be a personal fact."[26] Unfortunately, however, while admitting to this truth, many of those emphasizing the moral influence view tend to explain away the brutal facts of Christ dying for sin on the cross in the sense that His death turned aside (propitiated) divine wrath (judgment). Thus the end result of the moral influence approach is to rip away the foundation that puts forgiveness and love on a moral basis.

On the other hand, once we understand the cross in its primary functions as a substitutionary sacrifice and as a justification of God in His handling of the sin problem, then the positive emphasis of the moral influence theory, with its teaching that Jesus died to show us God's love and to inspire us to be like Him, makes good sense within the perspective of the New Testament. In other words, the moral influence approach to the work of Christ is wrong not in what it affirms, but in what it denies.

The fault, however, is not all on one side. While liberal theologians often have slighted the objective function of the cross, Evangelicals have tended to place too much emphasis on what Christ did for us on the cross without enough emphasis on what He does in human lives. Thus John Macquarrie is correct in his criticism when he writes that "objective views of the atonement do not sufficiently stress the existential dimension. Man cannot be saved as, let us say, a burning building can be saved, by an action that is entirely external to him. . . . Man is saved only in so far as he responds to and appropriates into his existence the saving activity that is directed toward him."[27]

While it is true that Christ's work of atonement is something He did and is doing for us by His death, resurrection, and heavenly ministry, it is also the case that His work cannot be completed without what He must do within us. "The atonement," writes J. K. Mozley, "whatever it be, must directly affect man in his moral life. Whatever else it may be it is only completed as it functions within man, as it is seen to be the at-one-ment of man with God." Thus Christ's work of at-one-ment encompasses both a divine act for humanity, and a human reaction in believers.[28] Beyond bringing believers back to oneness with God, a major purpose of the at-one-ment is the healing of the human relationships that the Fall fractured.

Within that framework of understanding, we need to see Christ's life as a pattern for our own. His life of obedience to God and His caring ways toward both His friends and enemies are an object lesson of what God would like to make out of every human life. Ellen White repeatedly mentions that Christ did not receive divine power in a way different from that which God gives it to us. Yet, she asserts, "we can never equal the pattern," even though "we may imitate and resemble it."[29]

The truth of the moral influence theory of Christ's work is that God did reveal His love through sending Christ and that that love does inspire us to live the loving life of the Master. Even that insight, however, must be applied with wisdom and discretion. J. M. Campbell has offered a helpful caution to those seeking to follow Christ's example by suggesting that Christians must take care not to live the life of sonship "as independent beings . . . following the example of the Son of God, but as abiding in the Son of God, as branches in the true vine."[30]

There is all the difference in the world between trying to be a Christian by following Christ's example and being a Christian through uniting with Him. Those two positions may sound like the same thing at first, but one smacks of salvation by works, while the other reflects the New Testament teaching that the believer must rely on Christ's empowering grace. Only the latter route leads to the fruit of the Spirit that makes Christians, in the words of Nietzsche, "look more redeemed" than they often do.

What the world needs is not more religiosity seeking to pass as Christianity, but more of the genuine item. "By this," Jesus told His disciples, "shall all men know that ye are my disciples, if ye have love one to another" (John 13:35, KJV). That kind of love takes place only when men and women unite their wills with the Christ of the cross and let Him live out His principles in their daily existence.

The Cross and the Life of the Church

The cross not only influences every aspect of an individual's daily life, but it also impacts upon the church in all its facets. That is not surprising, since Christ's saving work on the cross brought the church into being, and it continues to have relevance only as it proclaims the message of the cross.

The New Testament knows of no isolated Christianity. Christians, by definition, are those whom God has called out of "the world" to unite

The Cross of Christ

with like believers in fellowship and mission. Peter depicts the church as a spiritual house, with Christ as the cornerstone and His followers as living stones built into the unified structure (1 Peter 2:4-8; cf. Eph. 2:17-22). The disciple also describes Christians as citizens of a holy nation (1 Peter 2:9, 10).

One of Paul's favorite similes for the church is the body of Christ. Christ is the head, while the believers, with their diverse gifts, are likened to the various parts of the body (Eph. 1:22, 23; 4:12; 1 Cor. 12:12-26). We might ideally define the church as the community of believers who have responded to the cross.

As a result, the cross is central in genuine Christian worship. The Christian community is one united in celebrating salvation from the condemnation and power of sin, an element especially prominent in the great hymns of the Christian tradition, which base much of their imagery on the atoning work of Christ. Such hymns are a continuation of the heavenly anthems of praise to God found in the book of Revelation, which we examined in chapter 6. Worshipful praise is the spontaneous outflow of those who realize what God through Christ has done for the universe and for them personally and corporately. It is no accident that many of the great hymns of the church came from some of the foremost preachers of the cross, such as Martin Luther and the Wesleys.

Perhaps the richest symbolism for worship occurs in the holy Communion service. It is of interest to note that churches that violently differ over doctrine and worship unite in viewing the Communion service (thought of in terms of the Mass or the Eucharist by some denominations) as *the* central feature in Christian worship. But that is not surprising, however, when we realize that it is the only regular commemorative act authorized by Jesus. Certainly its impressive symbolism of His body "broken" for us and His blood "poured out for many for the forgiveness of sins" focuses the church on the centrality of Christ's death for the Christian faith (Matt. 26:26-29; Luke 22:19, 20; 1 Cor. 11:23-26).

The Communion service is a constant reminder of why Christ died and an ongoing invitation to participate in the continuing work of atonement. The celebration of the Lord's Supper, Vincent Taylor claims, is another indication "that Jesus did not view His suffering as a work accomplished apart from the response of men." "The eating and drinking were, and still are," John Stott suggests, "a vivid acted parable of receiving Christ as our crucified Saviour."[31] It ought to be the high point in a believer's worship experience.

Radical Faith's Response to the Cross

The cross of Christ must also be central in the Christian sermon. The ever-present theme of apostolic preaching was that "Christ died for our sins," a declaration usually tied to His victorious resurrection (1 Cor. 15:1-4; Acts 2:23, 24). It was those truths that made Christianity the force that it was and is. Tied to them was the preaching of sin and human need that drove people to both Christ's cross and their own crosses. When Christianity loses those themes, it forfeits its purpose for existence.

McGrath makes an excellent point when he says that the effort to make the cross "'more acceptable to the world'" is a "misguided attempt," because "it is through the proclamation of the cross that God finds his way back into a world from which he has been excluded."[32]

Without the cross, Christian preaching has nothing to add to the other moral systems, psychologies, and philosophies that permeate the world. Smooth Christian preaching that refuses to face the brutal facts of sin, sacrifice, Christ's cross, and our death with Him on our crosses has nothing to say to a world beset by alienation and death. Such preaching has no more word of hope than the optimistic fictions of humanistic psychology, and it certainly has no word of salvation. In what seems to be a meaningless universe, Christian preaching sets forth the cross as the key to meaning.

"The Son of God uplifted on the cross," Ellen White wrote, "is to be the foundation of every discourse given by our ministers."[33] One of the most impressive portrayals I have ever seen on the purpose of preaching was a painting I came across at the University of Wittenberg, where Luther began the Reformation. It was a simple picture, with Luther the preacher gazing upward and pointing toward the raised cross of Christ. On the other side of the painting the congregation was also staring upward at the cross. Neither preacher nor congregation was looking at each other. Both were focused upon the crucified Christ as Luther preached the gospel.

The cross not only impacts the internal life of a congregation, but also affects the attitudes and actions of that body of believers toward the non-Christian community in which it finds itself. Believers are "ambassadors for Christ" and He has entrusted them with "the ministry of reconciliation" (2 Cor. 5:19, 20). The very presence of the church in a community ought to lead not only to gospel preaching from the pulpit, but also to Christian betterment of both individuals and the society in which they exist. The church as reconciler is a healer and builder of relationships between individuals and God and between people.

Another important contribution of the cross to the life of the church is that it provides a meaningful framework in which to interpret and un-

The Cross of Christ

derstand the church's entire theological system. "The cross," McGrath stated, "is not just about one chapter of the Christian faith; it casts its shadow and stamps its form upon *all* of that theology." Ellen White set forth a similar perspective when she wrote that "the sacrifice of Christ as an atonement for sin is the great truth around which all other truths cluster. In order to be rightly understood and appreciated, every truth in the Word of God, from Genesis to Revelation, must be studied in the light that streams from the cross of Calvary."[34]

I would go one step further by suggesting that the philosophy of the cross provides a context for understanding all our knowledges, whether they be in the social sciences, the physical or life sciences, the humanities, or any other field. The grand central theme of Scripture (which includes the problem of sin, God's solution to it, and the conflict between Christ and Satan) provides a philosophic framework that makes sense out of the bits and pieces of knowledge that we glean from the empirical world around us. In fact, I would offer that the framework of the cross is the only satisfactory answer to understanding the mixed-up world in which we live.[35]

Given the centrality of the cross for the church, "the chief danger for the church," H. D. McDonald writes, "is that it should have within it those who are not of the gospel. This happens when the church becomes obsessed with niceness and numbers rather than with salvation and newness of life." Such members, he indicates, "may indeed have a taste for higher things, but have no taste of the highest." They will appreciate Christianity for its good ideas, and they will view it as a way of life, but they will stop short of it as a total "recasting of the soul."[36]

Thus the very facts of aging and success affect the nature of the church. It was so in the second-century church, and it has been the fate of every church since that time as the children and grandchildren of the "founding apostles" became more interested in institutional forms that are supposed to preserve the traditions, than in the dynamic, death-dealing, life-shattering cross itself.[37]

The Cross and Personal Tragedy

I sometimes wonder what happened to the little boy whom I visited in the Galveston burn clinic, the little fellow who fed himself with his right foot because he had no arms, the "innocent child" who had no eyelids, lips, or ears (see chapter 1). And as I visited the home of Anne Frank in Amsterdam, I wondered about the families of the millions who met their deaths under the fists of Hitler, Stalin, and their kin. In many ways, Satan's work seems to be more evident in the world around us than does God's.

Where was God when the little boy burned and when the Nazis murdered Slavs and Jews by the millions? How did He feel, and does He even have feelings? And if He is all-powerful and all-wise, why doesn't He put an end to all the suffering and injustice that we see around us? Sometimes God appears to be more like a moral iceberg in the sky than a Being who cares about the hurts and struggles of His children on earth.

It is difficult to sit by the bed of a loved one wasting away with terminal cancer without questioning the "caringness" and the goodness of God. I can handle death in the abstract. It doesn't overly affect me when I read that a mining accident asphyxiated 1,000 Mongolian miners. After all, I don't know any Mongolian miners. I can spin fine intellectual theories to account for such "meaningless" deaths, but I am shaken to the depth of my emotional being when crisis hits close to home, when it touches those I love. At such times the old doubts about God's goodness spontaneously resurrect.

The answer to these doubts is once again found in the cross of Christ. The cross demonstrates that God is not an infinite iceberg unconcerned with the pains of humanity. The cross is "God with us" in our suffering. On the cross He met suffering, loneliness, and death in human form in the person of Christ. Thus the cross is the symbol of God's relevance to our lives in a broken world in which Satan is still busy demonstrating the principles of his kingdom.

"Brotherhood with Christ," Moltmann indicates, "means the suffering and active participation in the history of this God."[38] Perhaps we have the picture backward. Some people have seemingly confused God with Hollywood's version of the U.S. Cavalry, a force for good that often arrived for the rescue right before the Indians overwhelmed the wagon train.

The reality is that neither Christ nor the apostles escaped suffering or painful deaths. They endured the outworkings of Satan's death-inflicting machinations in their lives. Christ told them that that would be their fate (John 15:18, 20; 16:1, 2). He made no empty promises. The all-knowing God never offered Christians an escape from life's problems, but He did promise them courage and support to meet crises and that they would have victory in the end. "In the world," Jesus told His disciples, "you have tribulation; but be of good cheer, I have overcome the world" (John 16:33).

The cross does away with any vision of God's rescuing us from all trouble. "At Calvary," McGrath reminds us, "God entered into the darkness of human pain and suffering. God faced the threat of extinction—and

The Cross of Christ

having met it, having recognized [sic], exposed and named it as it really is, he conquered it." The picture of Christ given at Calvary is one of a "deserted, bruised, bleeding and dying God, who lent new meaning and dignity to human suffering by passing through its shadow himself."[39] Christ is "a merciful and faithful high priest," we read in the book of Hebrews, "because he himself has suffered and been tempted." He is therefore able to help us in our times of trouble (Heb. 2:17, 18).

The good news of the gospel is that Christ not only suffered and died like other humans, but that He overcame death itself. Christ's resurrection victory is the guarantee that Satan has been defeated and that those who believe in Jesus will be resurrected to immortality when He comes again (1 Cor. 15:20-23, 51-56). Our sufferings become more manageable in the light of His victory. Since the time of His resurrection, Christians still suffer and die, but with the firm assurance that suffering and death are not the ultimate reality.

When we experience the loneliness of pain or when our closest friends forsake us and we feel deserted by God, we need to remember that Christ was there before us. The cross illuminates the human experiences of suffering, abandonment, powerlessness, and hopelessness. It teaches us, Luther wrote, "to believe in hope even when there is no hope."[40]

The Christian has been called not only to participate in the sufferings of Christ, but also to join Him in His resurrection. "The way of faith leads through the cross to the resurrection." The resurrection transforms the meaning of Christ's suffering on the cross, which makes the cross into a symbol of life and hope rather than one of suffering and death. Thus, writes McGrath, "through faith we are assured that the destiny of the one who was crucified and raised is *our* destiny—we learn to read *our* personal history into the story of the cross."[41]

The Christian by faith finds hope where others experience only hopelessness and boundless despair. The theology of the cross is a theology of hope. Because of the hopefulness of Christianity, Ellen White can write that "a life in Christ is a life of restfulness. There may be no ecstasy of feeling, but there should be an abiding, peaceful trust."[42]

Christ did not leave His disciples alone when He ascended to heaven. He sent to them the Holy Spirit to comfort and guide them. Accompanying the gift of the Spirit was the promise that His followers would have spiritual peace (John 14:26, 27). "The fruit of the Spirit," resulting from Christ's work on the cross, is "love, joy, peace, patience, kindness, goodness, faithfulness, gentleness, self-control" (Gal. 5:22, 23).

Radical Faith's Response to the Cross

Because of that "fruit," the Christian faces life, suffering, and death in a different state of mind than do those who have "no hope" (1 Thess. 4:13). As believers in Christ, we can look "to Jesus the pioneer and perfecter of our faith, who for the joy that was set before him endured the cross" (Heb. 12:2) as our example of victory in every adversity.

The cross of Christ is the answer to both our human problems on earth and the cosmic dilemma of sin. As Christians we look forward to that day when the experiment of sin is completed and it is "really finished." On that day the universe will declare that "salvation belongs to our God who sits upon the throne, and to the Lamb" (Rev. 7:10). God's aim all along has been to bring about through the cross the time when "there shall be no more death, neither sorrow, nor crying," nor "pain: for the former things are passed away" (Rev. 21:4, KJV).

---

[1] C. S. Lewis, *Mere Christianity* (New York: Macmillan, 1960), p. 56.

[2] Denney, *Christian Doctrine of Reconciliation*, p. 163.

[3] Martin Luther, *Greater Catechism*, quoted in Aulén, *Christus Victor*, p. 105.

[4] Denney, *Studies in Theology*, p. 155; Denney, *Christian Doctrine of Reconciliation*, p. 303 (cf. pp. 163, 164); Denney, *Death of Christ*, p. 128. (Italics supplied except in last sentence.)

[5] Moltmann, *The Crucified God*, p. 39.

[6] Forsyth, *Justification of God*, p. 126. (Italics supplied.)

[7] Dietrich Bonhoeffer, *The Cost of Discipleship* (New York: Collier Books, Macmillan, 1963), p. 99.

[8] Barclay, *Gospel of Matthew*, vol. 2, p. 167.

[9] H. H. Farmer, quoted in F. W. Dillistone, *The Significance of the Cross* (Philadelphia: Westminster, 1944), p. 155.

[10] White, *Steps to Christ*, pp. 47, 43; Denney, *Christian Doctrine of Reconciliation*, p. 198.

[11] Ellen G. White, *Thoughts From the Mount of Blessing* (Mountain View, Calif.: Pacific Press, 1956), p. 114.

[12] Dederen, "Atoning Aspects in Christ's Death," p. 314.

[13] Donald G. Bloesch, *Essentials of Evangelical Theology*, (San Francisco: Harper and Row, 1978), vol. 1, p. 164.

[14] Forsyth, *Justification of God*, p. 221.

[15] Heppenstall, *The Man Who Is God*, p. 168.

[16] Moltmann, *The Crucified God*, p. 71.

[17] Morris, *The Cross in the New Testament*, pp. 390-392; see also Walker, *Gospel of Reconciliation*, p. 189.

[18] Bonhoeffer, *The Cost of Discipleship*, p. 53.

[19] Denney, *Christian Doctrine of Reconciliation*, pp. 297, 300.

[20] Mildred Bangs Wynkoop, *A Theology of Love: The Dynamics of Wesleyanism* (Kansas City, Mo.: Beacon Hill Press of Kansas City, 1972), p. 233.

[21] James S. Stewart, *A Man in Christ* (New York: Harper and Brothers, n.d.), p. 196.

[22] McGrath, *Mystery of the Cross*, p. 155; White, *Steps to Christ*, p. 24.

[23] Friedrich Nietzsche, quoted in Provonsha, *You Can Go Home Again*, p. 106.

[24] Walker, *Gospel of Reconciliation*, p. 210.

[25] See Taylor, *Jesus and His Sacrifice*, pp. 299-303.

[26] R. C. Moberly, *Atonement and Personality* (London: John Murray, 1924), p. 143.

[27] Macquarrie, *Principles of Christian Theology*, p. 316.

[28] J K. Mozley, *The Doctrine of the Atonement* (London: Duckworth, 1915), p. 211; Tillich, *Systematic Theology*, vol. 2, p. 170.

[29] Ellen G. White, MS 21, 1895; Ellen G. White, *Review and Herald*, Feb. 5, 1895, p. 81. For a fuller treatment of this topic, see my *From 1888 to Apostasy* (Washington, D.C.: Review and Herald, 1987), pp. 132-150.

[30] See George Smeaton, *The Doctrine of the Atonement as Taught by Christ Himself* (Grand Rapids: Zondervan, 1953), pp. 412, 413; John McLeod Campbell, *The Nature of the Atonement*, 6th ed. (London: Macmillan, 1886), p. 173.

[31] Taylor, *Jesus and His Sacrifice*, p. 313; Stott, *Cross of Christ*, p. 70.

[32] McGrath, *Mystery of the Cross*, p. 116.

[33] White, *Gospel Workers*, p. 315.

[34] McGrath, *Mystery of the Cross*, p. 187; White, *Gospel Workers*, p. 315.

[35] For a fuller treatment of this topic, see my *Myths in Adventism* (Washington, D.C.: Review and Herald, 1985), pp. 127-151.

[36] McDonald, *Atonement of the Death of Christ*, p. 16.

[37] For more on the dynamics of an aging church, see Derek Tidball, *The Social Context of the New Testament: A Sociological Analysis* (Grand Rapids: Zondervan, 1984), pp. 123-136; Thomas F. O'Dea, *Sociology and the Study of Religion* (New York: Basic Books, 1970) pp. 240-255; David O. Moberg, *The Church as a Social Institution* 2d. ed. (Grand Rapids: Baker, 1984), pp. 119-124; George R. Knight, *If I Were the Devil: Seeing Through the Enemy's Smokescreen: Contemporary Challenges Facing Adventism* (Hagerstown, Md.: Review and Herald, 2007), pp. 26-31; 41-54.

[38] Moltmann, *The Crucified God*, p 338.

[39] McGrath, *Mystery of the Cross*, pp. 120, 157.

[40] Martin Luther, *Heidelberg Disputation*, quoted in McGrath, *Mystery of the Cross*, p. 9.

[41] McGrath, *Mystery of the Cross*, pp. 176, 107.

[42] White, *Steps to Christ*, p. 70.

A Final Word to the Reader

The subject matter of this book has not been the easiest to understand, but it is safe to say that there is no more important topic. The concept of atonement is basic to a Christian understanding of history, theology, and every other field of knowledge.

All human beings confront two great themes in their personal lives: (1) life is delightfully good, and people are obviously made for happiness and health, and (2) life is unbearably bad, and happiness, health, and even life itself deteriorate into misery, sickness, and death. The basic facts of life, they form the context in which all human activity takes place. Thus in our daily experience we are confronted with the inescapable reality of the great controversy between good and evil.

Such a state of affairs leads people to question the meaning of life and the goodness of a God who claims to be love, yet who permits the Hitlers, Stalins, Satans, and the more impersonal forces of destruction to continue operating with seeming impunity. We are all affected, and we all have our questions. Each person has a problem with God in one form or another.

The surprising part of the predicament of sin is God's solution to it. The most unlikely story in the universe is that of the cross. The concept of the "crucified God" is so improbable that it wouldn't even make good fiction because it contains a plot that "normal" people wouldn't dream up on their own. Humans don't solve their problems through servanthood and the sacrifice of their "hero." Yet it is through that unexpected method that God in His wisdom has made Himself known to the universe, while at the same time providing Satan with the opportunity to demonstrate his principles.

The readers of *The Cross of Christ* have probably noted that it has not given a large place to humans in the work of atonement. The simple fact is that the plan of salvation is God's work, not humanity's. It was Christ who lived the perfect life as a human being and proved that God's law could be kept; it was Christ who died for every person by absorbing the death penalty that resulted from the broken law; and it is Christ who currently ministers in heaven on behalf of those who believe in Him and accept the merits of His death and resurrection.

Atonement is all of God. It began in grace (unmerited favor), and it will be finished in grace. Christ's work will stand whether or not any human beings accept it. The human part in the atonement is that of response—of accepting Christ's work with its privileges and responsibilities—rather than that of accomplishment.

What God is accomplishing *for* people through the work of Christ is all important. Without God's work *for* individuals, there could be no subsequent work *in* them. *The Cross of Christ* has focused on what God has done *for* a lost world and a universe in doubt. Its companion volume, *Sin and Salvation*, continues the story of what God does *for* people but moves beyond to what God is willing to do *in* those who accept His offer of grace.

Some readers may think that this book should have included an exposition of the 144,000 of Revelation, who are "redeemed from the earth" (Rev. 14:3) as God's "spotless" ones (verse 5) and who are pictured as keeping "the commandments of God and the faith of Jesus" immediately prior to the Second Coming (verse 12). The second volume in this series will treat that topic since it deals with God's work *in* human beings. Their "spotlessness" and "faithfulness" are not a part of the atonement, but the result or fruit of God's atonement in Christ.

The Bible never gives humanity too prominent a place in the plan of salvation. The great controversy is between God and Satan, not Satan and humanity. Whether or not any human being ever demonstrates God's power in living a "spotless" life, the atonement will have been completed through the demonstration of Christ's sinless life, death, resurrection, and heavenly ministry. His sinless life is the great fact of the ages; His death demonstrated the principles of both God's and Satan's kingdoms; His heavenly ministry extends the fruits of His accomplished victory to those who have faith in Him; and His comings at the beginning and end of the millennium will complete the work of atonement. The biblical message is that salvation is from God alone.

As a result, the great heavenly songs recorded in Revelation have no place for the glorification of created beings in any way, no matter how pure their lives. Even the "spotless" 144,000 focus their praise totally on the work of God the Father and the Lamb. At the end of time, when Christ's work has irrefutably established God's justice, the whole universe will proclaim that "salvation and glory and power belong to our God, for [because] his judgments are true and just" (Rev. 19:1, 2; cf. 7:10).

Index of Biblical References

GENESIS
Page
1:29 45
2:17 36
3:1-6 .... 19, 20
3:4 117
3:7-10 .... 29, 34
3:8-10 30
3:11-13 131
3:12 31
3:13 31
3:17-19 32
3:18 45
3:21 .... 29, 45
3:22-24 36
3:24 41
4:1-7 .... 17, 45, 46
6:5-8 41
18:25 23
32:20 63

EXODUS
6:6 68
22:22-24 37
32:8-10 37
34:6 .... 42, 63

LEVITICUS
1:4 47
4:29 47
16 99
16:21 47
17:11 47
25:1 72
25:25 68
25:47-49 68

NUMBERS
16:1-40 41

DEUTERONOMY
21:23 .... 53, 57
27:26 53
32:36 99

RUTH
4:1-10 68

2 Kings
3:26, 27 63
16:3 63
21:2, 6 63

2 CHRONICLES
26:16-21 41

NEHEMIAH
9:17 63

JOB
21:20 37

PSALMS
7:12 40
51:3, 4 110
51:4 54
51:7 35
73 23

PROVERBS
17:15 73

ISAIAH
1:16-18	35
2:2	86
14:12-14	20
51:17	90
53:6-12	53
59:2	32
65:17-19	114

JEREMIAH
3:17	86
6:11-15	37
7:31	63
17:9	32
19:4-6	63

EZEKIEL
8:17, 18	37
18:4	47
18:20	22, 52
23:27	37
23:33, 34	90
28:17	20

DANIEL
7:10	99, 110, 111
7:22	99
7:22-27	104
7:26	99
8:11	98
12:1	111

MICAH
6:7	63

MALACHI
3:1-4	86
4:1	117

MATTHEW
2:1-18	85
4:3, 4	85
4:5-7	85
4:8-10	86
5:22	38
5:43-48	131
6:9	75
6:14	54
7:12	126
7:21-23	108
7:21-27	130
10:28	38
10:34-39	124
12:27, 28	89
12:31-34	89
12:38	86
14:22, 23	87
16:16-23	88
16:21	49
16:24	49
16:24, 25	124
16:27	99, 100, 104
18:33, 34	54
19:27	16
19:28	108
20:1-16	15, 16, 109
20:6	112
22:37	28, 131
22:39	126, 131
24:51	38
25:31-46	16, 17, 99, 108
26:26-29	134
26:28	49, 50
26:36-46	89
26:42	91
26:45, 46	91
26:53	93

Index of Biblical References

27:44 110
27:50, 51 94

MARK

3:5 38
6:7-13 83
8:31, 32 49
8:34 49
9:30-32 49
10:32-34 49
10:43-45 131
10:45 69
14:24 49
14:32-42 89
14:33, 34 89
15:29-32 92
15:33 94
15:34 .... 50, 93
15:37 94

LUKE

6:31 126
9:1-6 83
9:23 126
9:24 127
10:25-37 131
14:25-33 124
15 .... 13-15, 109
15:20-23 75
15:22 29
19:10 62
20:35 108
22:19, 20 134
22:37 53
22:39-46 89
23:34 93
23:36 92
23:39-43 110
23:46 94

JOHN

1:1 82
1:3 82
1:12 .... 74, 75
1:14 82
1:29 .... 46, 48
3:3 .... 36, 75
3:5 75
3:5, 6 36
3:16 .... 25, 66, 99
3:16, 17 62
3:36 .... 38, 40, 64, 67, 91, 99, 100
5:19 83
5:22-24 100
5:28, 29 .... 99, 104
5:30 .... 83, 104
6:14, 15 87
6:31 87
6:56 75
8:28 83
8:34 .... 34, 68
8:44 72
10:11 92
10:17, 18 92
12:25 124
12:27 49
12:31 95
13:1 49
13:35 .... 131, 133
14:1-3 104
14:10 83
14:26, 27 138
14:30 84
15:5-7 75
15:5-10 130
15:10 84
15:13 65
15:18-20 137
16:1, 2 137

145

16:11 20
16:33 137
19:30 94

ACTS
2:23, 24 ....58, 97, 135
3:15 ....58, 77
4:10 97
5:1-11 41
9:33-41 83
14:8-10 83
20:9, 10 83

ROMANS
1:4 97
1:18 38
1:21 38
1:26-28 40
2:5 38
2:8 38
2:12, 13 130
2:17 38
3:4 110
3:19 38
3:21-26 ....66, 110
3:23 ....28, 64, 71, 84
3:23-26 62
3:24-26 ....69, 71, 72, 115
3:25 ....64, 66, 72, 74, 78, 98
3:25, 26 ....66, 72, 73
3:26 ....23, 56
4:5 71
4:25 53
5:1 ....71, 75, 91
5:2 75
5:6 ....71, 73
5:8 71
5:9 ....40, 71, 78
5:9-10 91

5:10 ......30, 62, 71, 73, 74, 96, 97
5:12 ....34, 36
5:15 84
5:15-19 83
5:17 36
5:19 84
6:1-11 98
6:4, 5 127
6:9 97
6:11 ....74, 127
6:16 ....33, 68
6:23 ..20, 28, 36, 51, 71, 109, 117
7:15 98
7:21-24 34
8:1 ....65, 75
8:4 98
8:23 ....70, 77
9:14-18 17
12:1, 2 129
12:2 127

1 CORINTHIANS
1:9 75
1:18 57
1:22 86
1:23 57
1:23, 24 52
1:30 75
2:14 34
4:9 110
5:7 48
6:2, 3 108
6:18-20 69
10:16 75
11:23-26 134
12:12-26 134
15:1-3 ....53, 97
15:1-4 135
15:3 53

Index of Biblical References

15:3, 4	58
15:24	97
15:20-23	138
15:25	105
15:26	97
15:51-54	99, 104
15:51-56	97, 138

2 CORINTHIANS

1:12	34
5:14-21	53
5:17	75, 128
5:18-21	75
5:19	74
5:19, 20	62, 74, 135
5:21	25, 91, 93

GALATIANS

1:4	70
2:16	130
2:20	70, 71, 98, 128
3:10	53
3:13	25, 51, 53, 57, 69, 77, 91, 93
4:5	74, 75
5:16-26	98
5:22, 23	138

EPHESIANS

1:5	74
1:7	78
2:8	71
2:8, 9	130
2:14-16	75
2:16	74
2:17-22	134
4:12	134
4:22-24	127, 134
4:30	70, 77

5:2	70
5:25	70
6:12	19, 22, 119

PHILIPPIANS

2:5-8	82, 83, 85, 92, 128
2:8	85, 86
2:10, 11	119
2:12, 13	128
3:9	71
3:10	75
4:3	111

COLOSSIANS

1:16	82
1:20	19, 62, 74, 75, 78, 119
1:21, 22	30
2:8-15	127
2:14, 15	25
3:9, 10	127

1 THESSALONIANS

1:1	75
1:10	40
4:13	139
4:15-17	104
5:9, 10	40

2 THESSALONIANS

1:7-9	63

1 TIMOTHY

2:5, 6	69

TITUS

2:14	70, 77
3:3	34, 68

HEBREWS

1:2	82
1:1, 2	56, 97
1:3	76, 77
2:14	92
2:17, 18	138
4:15	21, 84, 85
4:16	98
7:25	77, 98
7:27	76
8:1-7	49
8:2	77, 78
8:5	78
8:31-35	98
9:11-14	76
9:12	67, 76
9:13, 14	76
9:22	46, 48
9:22, 23	76
9:23	48, 77
9:26	49, 67
9:26-28	76
9:28	100
10:2	76
10:4	49
10:9-14	93
10:10	67, 76
10:12	49
10:12, 13	97
10:12-14	67
10:22, 23	76
11:4	46
12:2	139

JAMES

2:17-20	130
3:2	34
3:7, 8	34
4:4	30

1 PETER

1:18, 19	48, 69, 70
2:4-10	134
2:11	34
2:24	21, 26, 53
3:18	53
5:8	96

2 PETER

3:12, 13	107, 120

1 JOHN

1:3	75
1:6	75
1:9	73, 77, 131
1:9-2:2	110, 115
2:1, 2	98
2:2	73
2:6	75
2:16	68
2:24	75
2:27, 28	75
4:10	25, 66
5:19	68

REVELATION

1:17, 18	97
2:26	108
3:18	29
3:21	108
4:11	115
5:4	115
5:9	69, 95, 115
5:12	95, 115
6:10	19
6:11	29
6:15-17	67

Index of Biblical References

6:16	38, 63	19:11-21	105, 106
6:16, 17	41, 100	19:17	105
7:1-4	103	19:19	105
7:9-12	120	19:19-21	104, 106
7:9-14	29, 95	20	104, 107
7:10	139, 142	20-22	75, 106
7:14	36	20:1	105
12:4	85	20:1-3	107
12:9	106	20:3	107
12:9, 10	95	20:4	105, 107, 108, 110
12:10, 11	99	20:4-9	105
13:6	98	20:7, 8	107
13:11-14:12	103	20:7-9	116
14:1-5	104	20:9	117
14:3-5	142	20:9-15	110
14:10	91	20:10	81
14:12	142	20:11, 12	111
15:3, 4	116	20:11-15	117
16:5	116	20:13-15	39
16:7	116	20:14, 15	81
16:10	107	20:15	117
16:12-16	106	21, 22	107
16:13-15	107	21:1	105
18:6	91	21:1-4	106, 120
19-21	105	21:4	114, 139
19:1, 2	116, 142	22:7	19
19:11	104, 105, 116	22:11	99

Index of Names and Topics

A

Abel, 17, 33, 45, 46
Abelard, Peter, 22, 52
Abraham, 22
Adam, 29-36, 45, 47, 73, 83, 127, 131
Adoption, 74, 75
Alienation, a result of sin, 30-33, 74; problem of answered by reconciliation, 73
Anger, at God's injustice, 14, 16, 17, 18
Annihilation, better than eternal misery, 115, 117, 118; of the wicked, 116-118
Anselm of Canterbury, 21, 52, 55
Armageddon, 106, 107, 116
Atonement, a complex topic, 10, 78; as a change in us, 50; as at-one-ment, 74, 120, 132; completely God's work, 141, 142; dividing line between theories of, 10; fully provided by God, 78; objective and subjective, 132, 133; process rather than a point, 10, 81, 82; theories of, 10, 11; see also, governmental theory of; moral influence theory of
Augustine, 70, 94
Aulén, Gustaf, 11

B

Baillie, D. M., 92
Barclay, William, 88, 94, 125
Barth, Karl, 73
Beast, mark of, 103
Berkouwer, G. C., 37, 67
Bloesch, Donald, 128
Blood, 17, 22, 45, 47, 49; as basis for all metaphors of salvation, 76-79; as ransom price, 69, 70; makes atonement, 48, 49
Boettner, Loraine, 21
Bonhoeffer, Dietrich, 93, 94, 96, 124, 130
Books of judgment, 111-115
Brunner, Emil, 36, 41, 51, 55, 73, 118, 119
Büchsel, Friedrich, 56
Bushnell, Horace, 50

C

Cain, 17, 33, 45, 46, 109
Caird, G. B., 107, 111
Campbell, J. M., 133
Campbell, R. J., 95
Cave, Sydney, 9
Christ, as God, 82; as intercessor, 98; as man, 82-84; as pattern, 132; as reconciler, 74; as redeemer, 68, 69; as sacrifice, 48; as sin bearer, 49, 74, 89, 91, 93, 94, 132; bore divine wrath, 64-66; bore human sin, 53-55,

58, 132; churches preach an emasculated, 122; could have escaped from cross, 92; could not see past the tomb, 93; could resume divine power at any time, 83; death made meaningful by His victorious life, 84; death of a demonstration of God's love, 50, 51, 119, 132; death of averts God's judgment, 51; death of central to Gospels, 49; died of broken heart, 94; died the second death, 94; dreaded the cross, 89; essential temptation was to "un-empty" Himself, 82-86, 91-95, 128; exhausted divine penalty for sin, 65; Godforsakeness of His death, 50, 57, 93, 94; heavenly ministry of, 97-100; His work of judgment, 99, 100; how He regarded His mission, 49; more than a great teacher and sinless example, 58; more than a moral hero or martyr, 93, 94; no middle ground in regard to, 122, 123; not liable to death penalty in Himself, 72; not pitted against an angry Father, 66; our justification, 71; preached a violent message, 122; resurrection of, 96-98; Satan had no authority over, 83, 95; second coming of, 100, 104, 106, 116; self-emptying of, 82-84; steps in work of, 81-120; temptations of, 82-91; tempted far beyond other humans, 84-86, 91; we are saved by His life, 96

Christianity, a death to old ways, 126; a new way of life, 126-133; a transformed life, 129; positive rather than negative, 127

Christus Victor, 11

Church, nature of, 133, 134

Clarke, William Newton, 52

Cleansing from sin, 35, 36, 76-78

Clow, W. M., 83

Coffman, Carl, 11

Coin, parable of lost, 13

Communion service, 134

Conversion, 125, 126

Covenant relationship, 73-75

Cranfield, C.E.B., 66

Cross, a stumbling block, 57; as judgment on sin, 26, 93; as revelation, 56, 72, 118; answer to pain and suffering, 136-138; center of all knowledge, 136, 141; center of Christian worship, 133-136; central and contextual to Christianity, 11, 56, 58, 88; Christ dreaded, 89; Christ's central temptation was to avoid, 85-88, 91; demonstration of God's holiness and justice, 26, 56, 65, 72, 95, 118; demonstration of God's love, 25, 26, 56, 62, 72, 95, 118, 131; demonstration of God's righteousness in justifying sinners, 115; demonstration of Satan's principles, 25, 56, 72, 95, 118; moral foundation for justification and forgiveness, 72, 74; moral necessity of, 65-67, 72, 118; one for every believer, 124-129; puts forgiveness on a moral foundation, 56, 67, 95, 118; symbol of death and shame, 56, 57, 125; symbol of defeat, 57, 96; the irreligious aspect of Christianity, 57; turning point of history, 95; why necessary, 54, 55

Cross and resurrection, basis of apostolic preaching, 57, 97, 135

Crucified God, the, 48-52

Crucifixion, broke last link of sympathy between unfallen worlds and Satan, 95; center of gospel, 51, 52; described, 56, 92, 125; most degrading form of death, 57: of the self, 123-129; turning point in great controversy, 11, 81, 82

Cullman, Oscar, 90

Cup, Christ's, 90; of wrath, 64, 90, 91

Curse, Christ became for us, 53

D

Dale, R. W., 40

Day of atonement, 46, 53, 99

Death, as the aim of Christ's life, 50; defined, 36; penalty for sin, 21, 28, 36, 55, 56; second, 110

Dederen, Raoul, 86, 127

Defilement, 35, 36

Denney, James, 37, 51, 64, 97, 123, 126, 130

Dillistone, F. W., 30

Dodd, C. H., 40

Doubt, Satan's avenue of attack, 19-21, 55, 116, 117

E

Eden restored, 106

Eve, 19-21, 29-36, 41, 45, 47, 83, 127, 131

Existence, three possible states of, 114

Expiation, see propitiation

F

Faith, a relationship with God, 129; abandonment of the soul to God, 123; leads to disharmony with the world, 123, 124; makes justification effective, 71; radical, 123, 124

Farmer, H. H., 126

Forgiveness, injustice of, 21, 22, 72, 109; moral basis of in the cross, 72, 73, 98; must be founded on holiness, 25, 26, 55, 66; must take divine wrath into consideration, 63, 64; related to blood, 46, 48

Forsyth, Peter T., 25, 26, 47, 54,

65, 66, 83, 93, 94, 118, 119, 123, 128
Frank, Anne, 136
Franks, Robert, 51
Free will, 28, 117, 118, 126
Freedom, myth of human, 33, 34
Freud, Sigmund, 33

G

Gerrish, B. A., 110
Gethsemane. 49; the apex of Christ's temptation, 89-91
God, as Cosmic Ruler, 55; distrust of a cosmic problem, 19, 55, 56, 66, 109; holiness of, 26, 55-57, 119, justice of, 67, 72, 115-120; justification of, 10, 23, 25, 66, 72, 73, 108, 113, 115-120, 142; love central to His character, 24; love of, 25, 26, 56, 66; love of must be balanced by justice, 55; nature of, 20, 21; not vindictive, 54; openness of, 110-115; penal action of against sin, 36, 64, 79 n. 8; Satan's accusations against, 19, 20; suffered with Christ on the cross, 66; vindication of, 23, 25, 110, 115-120, 142; wrath of, 36-42, 66
Goodness. natural, 33
Gospel, defined, 53
Gospels, abnormal biographies, 49, 50
Governmental theory of atonement, 20, 42, 71, 72, 118

Grace, appears to be immoral, 109; defined, 16, 109; God's, 29, 30, 71-75; not cheap, 70; stands at the basis of all the metaphors of salvation, 78, 79
Great Controversy, The, 11
Great controversy, in every human heart, 30, 31; is between God and Satan, 10, 142
Green, Michael, 54, 85, 89, 117
Gregory of Nyssa, 70
Grotius, Hugo, 20
Guillebaud, H. E., 24
Guilt, 29, 30, 64
Gulag Archipelago, 18
Gulley, Norman, 70
Gunton, Colon, 96
Guy, Fritz, 24

H

Hawthorne, Nathaniel, 35
Headlam, A. C., 64
Heart, transformation of, 126
Heaven, could be like hell, 114; who will be there, 117, 118
Heavenly sanctuary, a neglected doctrine, 97; Christ's ministry in, 76-78, 97-99; focal point of Satan's attacks, 98; God's command post, 98
Heim, Karl, 22
Hell, 117
Heppenstall, Edward, 11, 66, 67, 128
History, God's intervention in

course of, 36; most basic issue of, 22, 26; philosophy of, 10, 24
Hitler, Adolf, 18, 93, 103, 109, 117, 137, 141
Holiness, God's, 25, 26
Holy Spirit, 29, 83, 98, 129-131, 138
Hour, Christ's, 50, 89, 91
Humanity, helplessness of, 29, 30; problem of, 28

I

Incarnation, 82
Injustice, God's, 15-18, 52, 109, 136, 137, 141

J

John the Baptist, 48
Johnsson, William, 56, 76, 77
Josephus, 87
Judgment, aimed at getting people into heaven, 99; books of, 111-115; given to the saints during 1,000 years, 107; key concept in millennium, 105; millennial, 107, 110-120; post-millennial executive, 117; pre-Advent, 99, 104-111; pre-Advent turns upon one point, 17; purpose of millennial, 110, 113; surprises in, 108; to be completed before Second Coming, 99, 104
Judgment of sin, 47; Christ bore, 53, 54
Justice, God's, 15-26, 54, 55, 72, 115-120; human, 15, 16
Justification, 71-73; defined, 71; should not be separated from sanctification, 130
Justification of God, see God, justification of

K

Kenosis, Christ's, 82-84, 128; ours, 128
Koester, Craig, 78
Kruse, Colin, 73

L

Ladd, George Eldon, 71, 96, 104, 105, 108, 111
Lake of fire, 107, 117
Lamb, Revelation's, 29
Lane, William, 77
LaRondelle, Hans, 52
Last Supper. 89
Law, central to great controversy, 20, 21, 83; civil permits substitution, 54; criminal does not permit substitution, 54; Christ perfectly kept it, 84, 85, 92; expression of God's being, 21; God takes seriously, 55; internalization of principles of, 108, 118; must be upheld in atonement, 55, 72; penalty of broken met by justification, 71; Satan claimed it couldn't be kept, 83; to be established in perpetuity, 23
Lazarus, 97

Levitical system, 48, 52, 76, 77, 95, 99
Lewis, C. S., 25, 37, 109, 114, 122
Lex Talionis, 16
Lloyd-Jones, D. Martyn, 72
Lord's Supper, 134
Love, God's, 13, 14, 16; God's most basic characteristic, 24; God's must be balanced by justice, 55; God's is always in relation to holiness, 25, 26; the ultimate reality, 123
Lucifer, 20, 126
Luther, Martin, 53, 123, 130, 134, 135, 138

M

McDonald, H. D., 39, 42, 136
McGrath, Alister, 58, 131, 135, 136, 137, 138
Machen, J. Gresham, 53
Macquarrie, John, 52, 96, 132
Messiah, disciples needed new definition of work of, 88
Millennial judgment, purpose of, 110
Millennium, 104-120; a time of healing, 110, 111; defined, 105, 106; indispensable element in theology, 107
Moberly, R. C., 132
Moltmann, Jürgen, 22, 57, 58, 94, 123, 129, 137
Moral influence theory of atonement, 50, 51, 54, 93; strengths of, 132; weaknesses of, 51, 58, 65, 66, 93, 131, 132
Morris, Leon, 25, 30, 55, 64, 70, 72, 130
Mounce, Robert, 105, 107, 116
Mozley, J. K., 132
Murray, John, 49, 84
My Gripe With God, 11

N

Nakedness, 29-31, 34
Nature, human, 32-35
New birth, 36, 75, 126, 127, 131
Nietzsche, Friedrich, 131, 133

P

Packer, J. I., 37
Pain, problem of, 18, 19; the Christian and, 136-139
Pain and suffering, God experienced on the cross, 137, 138
Penal action of God against sin, 36
Penal suffering of Christ, 79 n. 8
Penalty for sin, Christ bore, 53-56, 64-66, 95, 119; met by justification, 71
Perfection, 16, 34
Peter, called Satan, 88, 124; identifies Jesus as Messiah, 88
Pharisees, 16, 17, 108
Polycarp, martyrdom of, 90, 94
Preaching, purpose of, 135
Probation, close of human, 99
Prodigal son, 13, 50, 51, 75, 109
Propitiation, 62-67; abuses of, 63; an unpopular teaching, 62;

defined, 63; flows out of grace, 66; not an appeasement of God's wrath, 66; proof of God's righteousness, 66; tied to reconciliation, 74; tied to redemption, 69; tied to wrath, 64

Punishment, cannot be transferred, 52

Purchase price, 68-70

Purification, from defilement, 35, 36, 76-78

R

Ransom, 68, 69

Rashdall, Hastings, 50

Reason, human is dividing line for theories of atonement, 10; weakness of human exposed by the cross, 58 Rebellion, Satan's a lesson book for the universe, 25, 117, 118

Reconciliation, 73-75; answers to problem of alienation, 73; defined, 74; ministry of, 135; results of, 75, 130, 133; tied to propitiation, 74

Redemption, 67-70; defined, 68; in Old Testament, 68; leads to service, 69

Redemption and Revelation, 11

Regeneration, 127

Relationship, central to justification, 71; central to sin, 54, 73

Resurrection, basis of apostolic preaching, 57, 97, 135; Christ's transformed disciples, 96, 97; of Christ, 96; of the saints, 104, 105, 138; of the human spiritual life, 126, 127; of the wicked, 104, 105, 116; symbol of Christ's victory over death, 96, 97

Rewards, parable of unjust, 15, 16

Rice, Richard, 39, 78

Richardson, Alan, 39

Righteousness, cannot be transferred, 52, 54; demonstration of God's, 25; God's questioned, 22

Robe, Christ's, 30

Robinson, H. Wheeler, 11, 22, 39, 47, 97

Rousseau, Jean-Jacques, 33

Ruler, rich young, 16

S

Sacrifice, a disgusting concept, 44, 45, 48; a result of God's grace, 47; Christ's, 48-52; Christ's is moral basis of forgiveness, 98; living, 129; meaning of, 47; meaning of never made explicit in Old Testament, 47; meaning of self-evident, 47; New Testament, 48-53, 54; Old Testament, 45-48, 52; see also, substitutionary sacrifice

Salvation by works, 29

Sanctification, should not be separated from justification, 130

Index of Names and Topics

Sanctuary, heavenly, see heavenly sanctuary
Sanday, William, 64
Sarte, Jean-Paul, 31
Satan, 19-22, 55, 68, 83-86, 88, 91, 99, 109, 110, 116-118, 137, 141; defeat of sealed at the cross, 95; demonstrated his principles at the cross, 25, 56, 72, 95, 96; destruction of, 106; has not conceded defeat, 96, 97, 103; his charges refuted, 119; reason not destroyed at time of the Crucifixion, 96; why God permits him to continue, 24
Scarlet Letter, 35
Seal, God's, 103, 104
Second coming of Christ, 100, 104, 106, 116
Self, warfare against is greatest battle, 126
Self-denial, 125
Self-love, true and false, 126
Service, Christian ethic of, 131; principle of Christ's kingdom, 122
Sheep, parable of lost, 13
Sheep and goats, parable of, 16, 17, 108,
Sin, a cosmic dilemma, 22, 23, 119; a divine crisis, 119; a serious matter, 65; a temporary defeat of God, 22; affects entire universe, 10; an attack on God's honor, 119; as rebellion, 14, 28, 46, 74, 125; cannot be transferred, 52, 54; Christ bore human, 54, committed against a person, 54; could theoretically rise again, 118; defined, 28, 30, 31, 73, 125, 126; distinguished from crime, 54; must be consciously sentenced to death, 125; must be judged, 55; results of, 29-42; touches all humans, 28, 34; will never arise again, 118, 119
Sinner, definition of, 30
Slave, definition of, 34
Slavery to sin, a result of the Fall, 33-35; internal, 68; related to redemption, 68
Socinians, 22
Socrates, death of, 90, 96
Solzhenitsyn, Aleksandr, 18
Son, parable of lost, 13, 50, 75, 109
Spirit, fruits of, 138
Stählin, Gustav, 38
Stalin, Joseph, 18, 109, 137, 141
Stalker, James, 52, 96
Stewart, James, 119, 130
Stott, John R. W., 34, 47, 55, 62, 73, 78, 79, 84, 90, 134
Substitution, basis of Reformation theology, 53; biblical, 52, 53; not permitted by criminal law, 54; permitted by civil law, 54; unethical, 21, 22, 52, 54
Substitutionary sacrifice, 17, 25, 44-58; central to Christianity,

61, 62, 78, 79, 94; injustice of, 21, 22; rejected by many scholars, 50; separates Christianity from all other religions, 58; "sub-Christian," 52
Substitutionary suffering, a problem, 52
Suffering, human is more bearable in light of the cross, 138
Surrender, 126-128
Swete, H. B., 111

T

Taylor, Vincent, 47, 71, 74, 81, 82, 83, 120, 134
Tears, during the millennium, 113, 114
Temptation, Adam and Eve's, 20; Christ's, 81-91; Christ's centered on avoiding the cross, 85-88, 91; Christ's was to use His divine power for Himself, 83-86, 92, 93, 95, 128; human is to be self-reliant, 128
Theories of the atonement, 10, 11
Tillich, Paul, 55

U

Universe, moral stability of, 20

V

Vindication of God, 72, 73

W

Walker, W. L., 74, 131
Warfield, Benjamin, 51, 58
Weatherhead, Leslie, 51, 86
Wenham, Gordon, 47
Wenham, John, 117
Wesley, John and Charles, 134
Whale, J. S., 48
White, Ellen G., 11, 21, 23, 24, 34, 46, 53, 55, 58, 66, 67, 69, 83-85, 94-96, 98, 114, 116, 118, 120, 126, 127, 133, 135, 136, 138
Wicked, destruction of an act of mercy, 117
Will, free, 28, 118; power of, 126; related to sin, 31, 118; surrender of, 126-128
Wilson, William, 50
Winslow, Octavius, 62
Works, human, 130; in the judgment, 130; salvation by, 29
Wrath of God, 36-42, 63; an unpopular teaching, 37; argument for impersonal or passive, 40; argument for personal and active, 40-42, 63; as judgment on sin, 64, 66; Christ bore the Christian's portion, 64-67; defined, 37-42, 63, 64; primarily eschatological, 40; rejectors of Christ remain under, 67
Wrath of Jesus, 38, 41, 63
Wynkoop, Mildred, 130

Y

Yancey, Philip, 18
Yoder, John, 83
Yom Kippur, 99

THE ADVENTIST PIONEERS

Stories You'll Love

Heartwarming Stories of Adventist Pioneers
Norma J. Collins

They spent their lives, their health, their pennies, and their fortunes on spreading the three angels' messages. Here are the stories of the inspiring men and women who devoted their lives to knowing and sharing truth.

You Will See Your Lord a-Coming
Paperback. 0-8280-1895-2.

Their Works Do Follow Them
Paperback. 978-0-8280-2014-5.

ADVENTIST PIONEER SERIES

John Harvey Kellogg
Pioneering Health Reformer
Richard W. Schwarz
Uncover the complicated and controversial life of J. H. Kellogg, a man who packed the accomplishments of many men into one lifetime.
Hardcover. 0-8280-1939-8.

W. W. Prescott
Forgotten Giant of Adventism's Second Generation
Gilbert M. Valentine
Examine how W. W. Prescott impacted the church's educational system, theology, and policies during a critical era.
Hardcover. 0-8280-1892-8.

Joseph Bates
The Real Founder of Seventh-day Adventism
George R. Knight
Learn about the man who gave his estate to the Advent movement and spent the rest of his life in unpaid service to his King.
Hardcover. 0-8280-1815-4.

James White
Innovator and Overcomer
Gerald Wheeler
Explore James White's personality, family, theology, and entrepreneurship—and discover how personality traits and events shaped White as a man and leader.
Hardcover. 0-8280-1719-0.

3 WAYS TO SHOP

Visit your local Adventist Book Center®
Call 1-800-765-6955 (ABC)
Order online at AdventistBookCenter.com

REVIEW AND HERALD® PUBLISHING ASSOCIATION
Since 1861 | www.reviewandherald.com

Price and availability subject to change. Canadian prices higher. Printed in U.S.A. Sale price in effect until September 30, 2007.

Enhance Your Bible Study
WITH GEORGE KNIGHT'S DEVOTIONAL COMMENTARY SERIES

These user-friendly devotional commentaries lead you step-by-step through the Bible. The format makes these books perfect for individual study, small groups, or midweek meetings.

(Download free study guides at AdventistBookCenter.com.
Go to book detail and click on the study guide icon in the upper-right-hand corner.)

EXPLORING HEBREWS
Hebrews' message of confidence in God and His promises has motivated millions to persevere in faith. The author leads you through one of the most relevant books in the Bible. Paperback. 0-8280-1755-7.

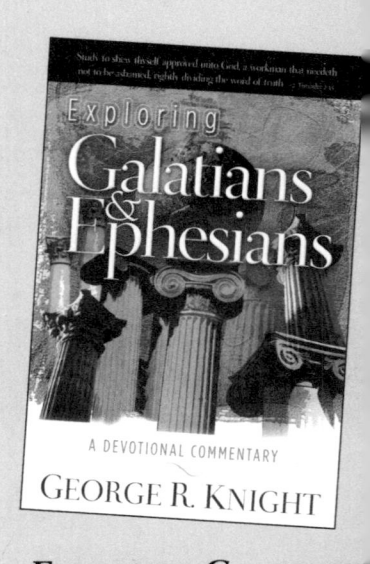

EXPLORING MARK
This book brings Mark's world down to us as we go behind the scenes and unfold the rich tapestry of Mark. Paperback. 0-8280-1837-5.

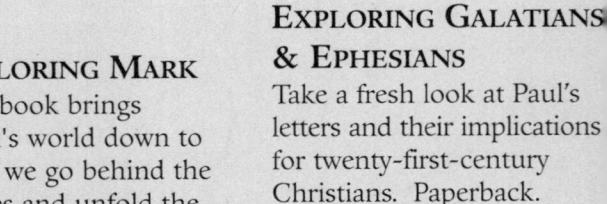

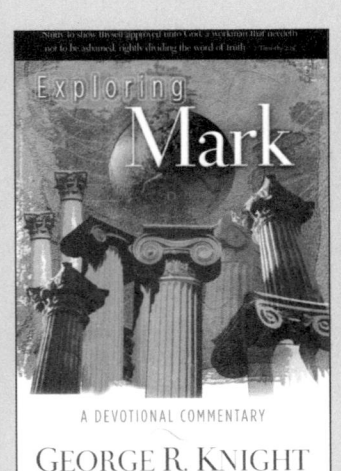

EXPLORING GALATIANS & EPHESIANS
Take a fresh look at Paul's letters and their implications for twenty-first-century Christians. Paperback. 0-8280-1896-0.

More books to come!
Watch for other great titles in the Exploring Devotional Commentary Series by George Knight. EXPLORING ROMANS will be released in 2007.

3 WAYS TO SHOP
- Visit your local **Adventist Book Center**®
- Call **1-800-765-6955**
- Order online at **AdventistBookCenter.com**

REVIEW AND HERALD® PUBLISHING ASSOCIATION